尾田栄一郎

Hello and thank you for taking our bus tour. We're heading toward the 100th chapter of *One Piece*. On your right, you can see the thumbs held up high. There's plenty more action and adventure ahead!

-Eiichiro Oda, 1999

WITHDRAWN

D1158758

E is manga career at the age of 17, when his one-shot cowboy manga **Wanted!** won second place in the coveted Tezuka manga awards. Oda went on to work as an assistant to some of the biggest manga artists in the industry, including Nobuhiro Watsuki, before winning the Hop Step Award for new artists. His pirate adventure **One Piece**, which debuted in **Weekly Shonen Jump** in 1997, quickly became one of the most popular manga in Japan.

ONE PIECE VOL. 11
EAST BLUE PART 11

SHONEN JUMP Manga Edition

This graphic novel contains material that was originally published in English in **SHONEN JUMP** #39–41.

STORY AND ART BY EIICHIRO ODA

English Adaptation/Lance Caselman
Translation/JN Productions & Michie Yamakawa
Touch-up Art & Lettering/Mark McMurray, Vanessa Satone
Additional Touch-up/Josh Simpson
Design/Sean Lee
Editor/Yuki Takagaki

ONE PIECE © 1997 by Eiichiro Oda. All rights reserved.
First published in Japan in 1997 by SHUEISHA Inc., Tokyo.
English translation rights arranged by SHUEISHA Inc.

The stories, characters and incidents mentioned in this publication are entirely fictional.

No portion of this book may be reproduced or transmitted in any form or by any means without written permission from the copyright holders.

Printed in the U.S.A.

Published by VIZ Media, LLC
P.O. Box 77010
San Francisco, CA 94107

10 9 8 7
First printing, July 2006
Seventh printing, April 2013

www.viz.com

www.shonenjump.com

3 1526 04564264 9

Vol. 11

THE MEANEST MAN IN THE EAST

STORY AND ART BY

EIICHIRO ODA

Nami
A thief who once specialized in robbing pirates. Although she hates pirates, Luffy convinced her to be his navigator.

Monkey D. Luffy
Boundlessly optimistic and able to stretch like rubber, he is determined to become King of the Pirates.

Usopp
His penchant for tall tales is matched by his accuracy with a slingshot. His father, Yasopp, is a member of "Red-Haired" Shanks's crew.

THE STORY OF ONE PIECE

Volume 11

Monkey D. Luffy started out as just a kid with a dream—and that dream was to become the greatest pirate in history! Stirred by the tales of pirate "Red-Haired" Shanks, Luffy vowed to become a pirate himself. That was before the enchanted Devil Fruit gave Luffy the power to stretch like rubber, at the cost of being unable to swim—a serious handicap for an aspiring sea dog. Undeterred, Luffy set out to sea and recruited some crewmates: master swordsman Zolo, treasure-hunting thief Nami, lying sharpshooter Usopp, and Sanji, the high-kicking chef.

Searching for Nami, Luffy and his crew head to Arlong Park, stronghold of the ferocious Fish-Man Pirates, only to discover that Nami herself is one of them! They learn the story of Belle Mère and the origin of Nami's hatred of pirates from Nami's stepsister, Nojiko, who also explains how Nami swallowed her hatred and went to work for Arlong, gathering loot to buy her village's freedom.

Moved by Nami's secret suffering, Luffy goes toe to toe with Arlong, but is hurled into the ocean! Sanji and the others fight and defeat Arlong's men and rescue Luffy. But they still have to contend with the most terrible foe of all—Arlong himself!

Sanji
The kind-hearted cook (and ladies' man) whose dream is to find the legendary sea, the "All Blue."

Roronoa Zolo
A former bounty hunter and master of the "three-sword" fighting style. He plans to become the world's greatest swordsman!

Vol. 11
THE MEANEST MAN IN THE EAST

CONTENTS

Chapter 91: Darts	7
Chapter 92: Happiness	27
Chapter 93: Going Down	47
Chapter 94: The Other Villain	67
Chapter 95: Spin, Pinwheel	85
Chapter 96: The Meanest Man in the East	105
Chapter 97: Kitetsu III	125
Chapter 98: Dark Clouds	145
Chapter 99: Luffy Died	165

Chapter 91: DARTS

KOBY AND HELMEPPO'S CHRONICLE OF TOIL
VOL. 8: "THE SHIP OF VICE ADMIRAL GARP"

HEY, YOU ATTACKED US FIRST.

HOW DARE YOU USE ONE OF MY MEN AS A SHIELD !!!

CHOMP CHOMP
CHOMP CHOMP
CHOMP CHOMP
TOOTH ATTACK !!!!
AAH!!
CHOMP
UGH!!
OOF!!
UNH...

GRAARR !!!
!!!
WHAK
THUD!!!
...!!!
I DID IT.
SHWOOM!!

LUFFY, ARE YOU NUTS!? THAT WAS YOUR BIG IDEA!?
LUF...
...ARE UNBREAKABLE!!?
AHHHH
...THAT MY TEETH ...
GRR...
DON'T YOU KNOW ...
SHU
NK!
CHONK
CHONK
NOW I HAVE SHARK TEETH, TOO !!!
LOOK!
SOME KEY TO VICTORY.

SH WAK!
HOW DARE YOU MOCK ME !!!
UGH !!!

AAAGH!! I'VE BEEN BEATEN BY A FISH!!!

CHONK
I'M NOT FOOLING AROUND !!
CHONK
!!
THAT'S WHAT YOU GET FOR FOOLING AROUND !!!

CHO
CHOMP
TOOTH ATTACK !!!!
WAAH!
CHOMP
UNH!
HUFF...
WH
AM!!
WH
OM!!
BWAH HA HA !!

CH
CHAP.!!!
YOW !!!
GRRA-AAARR !!!
THAT HAD TO HURT !!!
SH
UNK
RAAGH !!!!

HOW'S IT FEEL BEING BITTEN BY YOUR OWN TEETH!? HURTS, HUH!?
WA HA HA HA
ARLONG PARK
WHUMP!!
...!!!
!!!
...FLESH AND BONE !!!!
SHAKI!!
THEY MAY BE MY TEETH, BUT YOUR JAWS ARE TOO WEAK!
SHAK...
A SHARK'S TEETH ARE DEADLY BECAUSE ITS JAW MUSCLES HAVE THE STRENGTH TO BITE THROUGH...

SWUP...
!
AAAAAAAH !!!
KREK KREK !!!
NO!!! HE'LL BITE OFF LUFFY'S ARM!!!
GAH !!!
FWA
GRAAAH !!!!
!!!?

WHUMP....!!
...!!
SHLUP...
ARE YOU OKAY, LUFFY !!?
IF HE'D TAKEN ONE STEP BACK, HE WOULD'VE LOST THAT ARM!
I DOUBT HE KNEW THAT. IT HAD TO BE DUMB LUCK.
WOOOO
WOOOO
WOOOOO
...

SH LUK

DO OM!!!
HUH?
HUFF... HUFF...
WHERE'D HE GO !?

THE WATER ...

LUFFY, HE'S IN THE WATER !!!

WOOOOOOO
!
SSSSSSSS

WHAT ?
HE WENT UNDER.

GURGLE...

IT'S ARLONG !!!
HEY, A SHARK !!!
WHUP!

NOBODY CAN BEAT ME IN THE WATER! I'M EVEN FASTER IN MY OWN ELEMENT !!!

GLUP
GLUP

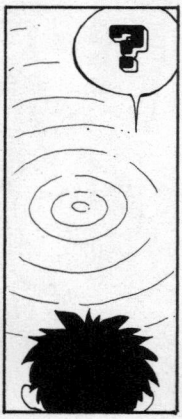
?

DA-DOOM
?
SHEEN!
SHARK ...
DID HE ESCAPE ?
WAAH !!!!
...DARTS !!!!

KRASH!!!
WHAT WAS THAT !!?
!!?
A TORPEDO !!?
!!!
ARLONG CAME OUT OF THE WATER!!!
!!?
THUD!!!
UNH...

WOOOO
HMM ...
YOU WITH-STOOD MY ATTACK.
WOO
OOOOOH...
plip plip...

...YOUR TORMENT CONTINUES !!!
SHE
EN
BUT THAT JUST MEANS...

SH
C!!
OM!!
SHARK DARTS !!!!

CH
UK
HAH!!
DO
OM!
HE'S GOT HIS NOSE STUCK IN THE GROUND !!!
huff
UGH!!
huff
THAT STINKING SHARK!
HE...HE REALLY IS UNBREAK-ABLE!!

OW !!!
SHARK DARTS !!!!
OOM
W OOO
UNGH !!!
WH
OOM!!
!
WOO
OO
!
LUFFY, HIDE!! ARLONG'S BACK IN THE WATER!!
FW
UMP
!!!
!!

NO WAY !!!

WHAT ARE YOU DOING!? HE'S GONNA ATTACK AGAIN!! RUN!!

NO.
plup
plup...

BROTHER LUFFY, YOU HAVE TO RETREAT!!
...

WOOOOOO
I'M GONNA KNOCK HIM OUT !!!
I'M GONNA GET HIM.

DOOM!

GLUP
DOOM!
GLUP

INSTEAD OF THE SBS QUESTION CORNER, HERE'S A CUT-AWAY VIEW OF LUFFY'S SHIP, THE *MERRY GO*. A LOT OF READERS HAVE ASKED ABOUT IT.

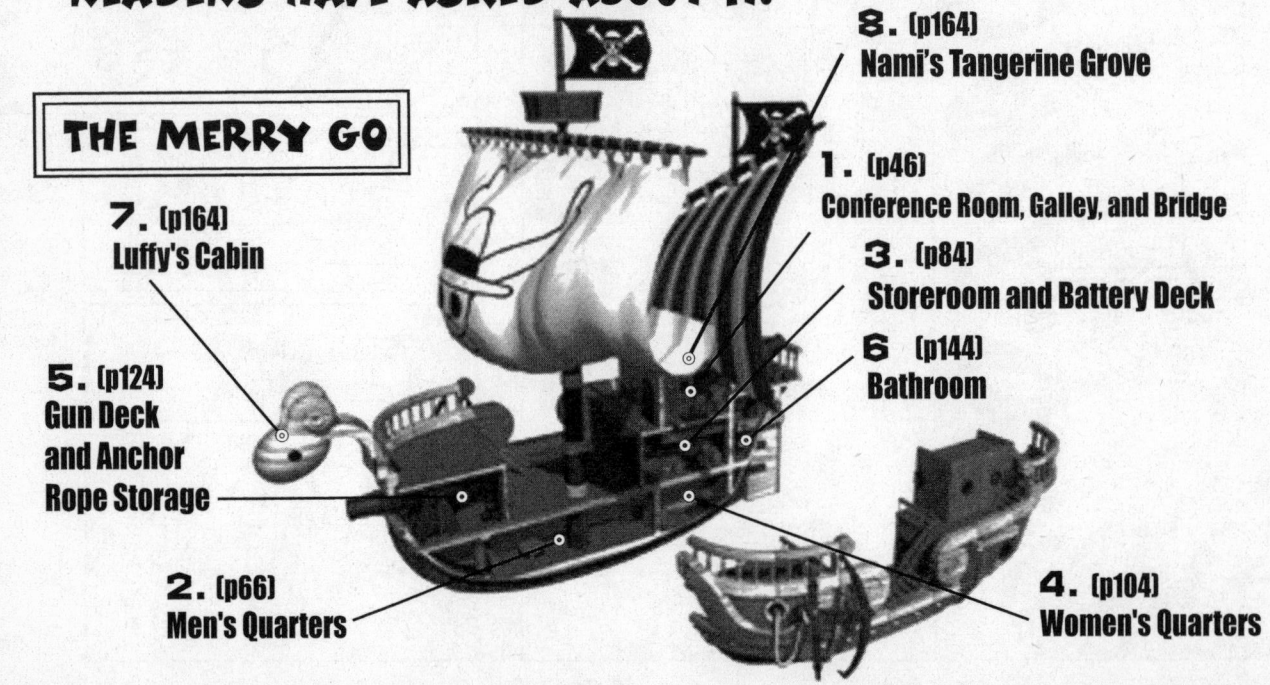

Chapter 92: HAPPINESS

KOBY AND HELMEPPO'S CHRONICLE OF TOIL, VOL. 9: "THE EXTRADITION OF MORGAN"

WOOOOOO

OR HAVE YOU GIVEN UP?
GLUP
YOU'VE GOT GUTS, HUMAN.
GLUP

COME ON...
WOOO
...YOU LOUSY SHARK !!!

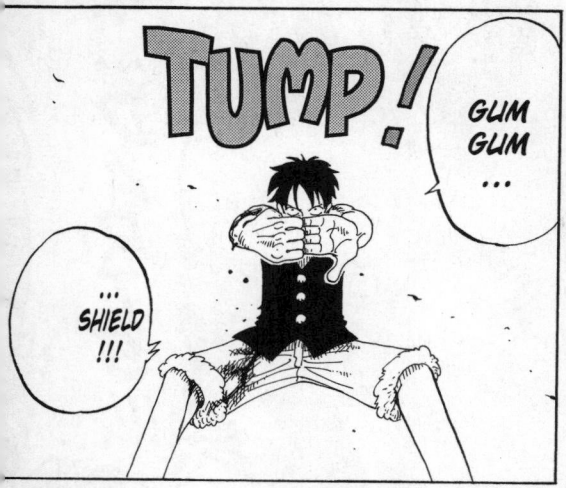
TUMP!
GUM GUM ...
... SHIELD !!!

YOU'RE TAKING THE FULL FORCE OF HIS ATTACKS!!
DON'T YOU UNDER-STAND WHAT "HIDE" MEANS, LUFFY!!?
IF HE HITS YOU AGAIN, YOU'RE DOOMED !!!

WOING

DOES HE THINK THAT'LL PROTECT HIM?
WHAT'S THAT?

SHARK...

SHWOO
I'LL SKEWER HIS WORTH-LESS HEART !!!
I'M GOING TWICE AS FAST THIS TIME !!!
OOOO

SHUN
K
...DARTS!!!!
UGH
....!!
!!?
NOOOOOO
BROTHER LUFFY'S HIT!!!
HEE!

BWOING
ARLONG PARK
WHA-BAM!!!
HE BOUNCED BACK !!!
NO!
WHAT HAPPENED !!? IS HE DEAD !!?
THWAK!!
THAT TRICK'S NOT GONNA WORK!!
HA HA HA! YOU'RE FINISHED, ARLONG!!

OOF !!!
SHARK DARTS !!!!
THWAM!!
YOU GOT LUCKY, YOU DIRTY SCOUNDREL !!!
YOU CAUGHT ME BY SUR-PRISE !!
skrsh
YOU CAN'T ESCAPE!
GET READY!! GUM-GUM...
BUT THIS'LL FINISH YOU !!!
WHOOM

...FINGER NET!!!
FW
AP!!
WHO
OSH!!
!?
I'M GOING FISHING!!
THWAP
AND...
...!!
!?
SHWUP...

SH
WA
...
SPEAR
!!!!
!!!!
WOOO.....
GAH
!!!

RA
AAH
IT WORKED !!!
HEY!!!
klink
WOOO
IS HE DEAD?
HUH?
HAAAA
KA-
SHUNG!!

I'VE NEVER SEEN EYES LIKE THAT!!
LUFFY'S ATTACK ONLY ENRAGED HIM!!!
THAT'S HOW THE FISH-MEN LOOK WHEN THEY GO BERSERK !!!
ARLONG LOOKS DIFFERENT !!
ARGH !!
KA-TH
WOW
YOU'RE A HUMAN, AN INFERIOR CREATURE !!!
AAAAAH !!
DWOI
NG!
AND I AM A MIGHTY FISH-MAN !!

!!!
TRASH
NOW YOU'LL PAY !!!!
WHOOM !!!
WOOO
EEK!
I'M NOT HURT, BUT HE SURE IS MAD.
THROB
THROB
HEY! YOU CAUGHT ME OFF GUARD AGAIN.
DO
OMG

BO
WHOA !!
WHAP!
SHEEN

!
KREESH..!!
THAT'S HIS SHARK SAW!!
IT'S A GIANT SAW !!!
WHAT'S THAT?

SHUNK
WAH!
WOOSH!
!!
WHOOM
FWUMP!!
OWW !!
OW!
WHAM!!
THWUMP!!

FWUMP
THUD
KRASH!!
LUFFY'S LOSING !!!
ARLONG'S RELENT-LESS !!!
STAND
HUFF
THO
OM!!
UGH!
HUFF
HUFF
KRASH!!
AGH !!
KRAK!!

THE CHART ROOM !!
...!!
WHEEZE WHEEZE
HUFF HUFF
THE TOP FLOOR, THE ROOM ON THE LEFT.
HE'S FLED INTO THE BUILDING!

WOOOOO
...LITTLE RUBBER MAN.
STAY OUT OF MY WAY ...

WHAT IS THIS PLACE?
HUFF
HUFF
AND ALL THIS PAPER?
krunch krunch ...

FISH-MEN ARE EXCELLENT AT GATHERING OCEANIC DATA, BUT WITHOUT A GOOD CARTOGRAPHER IT'S WORTHLESS.
THIS ISN'T JUST PAPER.
!
NO ONE ELSE IN THE WORLD CAN DRAW SUCH ACCURATE MAPS.
THESE ARE CHARTS. NAMI SPENT THE LAST EIGHT YEARS DRAWING THEM.

I SEE.

NAMI'S A GENIUS.

...HAS BLOOD ON IT.
THIS PEN ...
THERE'S NOTHING MORE TRAGIC AND STUPID THAN WASTING ONE'S GIFTS!!
...

SW UP!!
ONCE WE HAVE CHARTS OF ALL THE WORLD'S OCEANS, NOTHING CAN STOP THE FISH-MEN!!
THE WHOLE WORLD WILL BE MY KINGDOM !!!
DRAWING CHARTS FOR ME ALLOWS NAMI TO DO THE THING SHE LOVES BEST !!!
AND SOON I WILL ACHIEVE MY AMBITION !!!

THINK YOU CAN USE THAT GIRL AS WELL AS I DO!!?

I SEE ...

...THE EAST BLUE !!!
THIS ISLAND IS THE STEPPING STONE TO...

KLAK...
...WON'T MOVE !!!
WHAT!? MY SAW ...
!?
WOOo...!!
TUP...
DOOM!!
KREK KREK
"USE"?

1. Lounge

Conference Room, Galley, and Bridge

- Room for meetings and discussions
- The crew gathers here for meals and breaks.

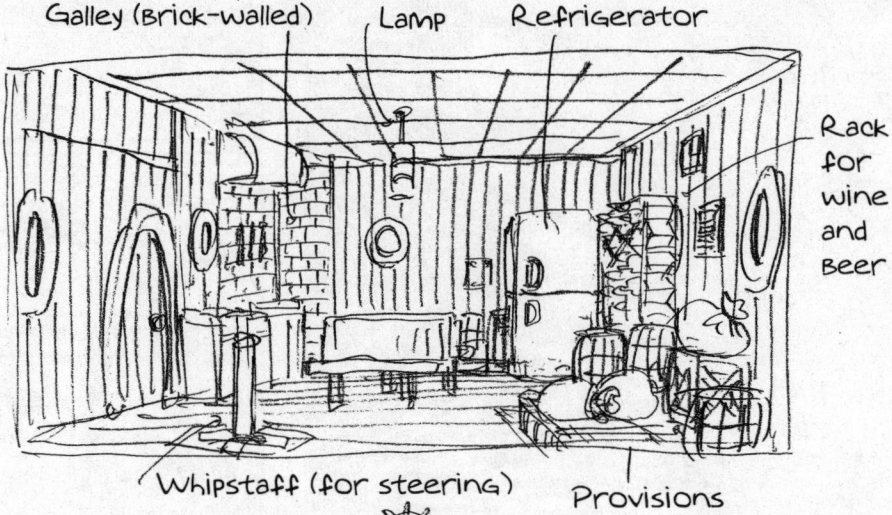

This ship isn't steered with a wheel. The whipstaff that's attached to the tiller turns the rudder and steers the ship right or left.

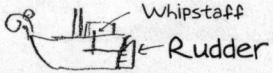

Chapter 93: GOING DOWN

KLANG

MY SHARK SAW... !!!
!!

...NAMI IS, ANYWAY?
WHAT DO YOU THINK...

SHE'S AN EXCELLENT CARTOGRAPHER, EVEN IF SHE IS OF AN INFERIOR SPECIES.
SHE'S RATHER LIKE A SPIRITED KITTEN...
COMPARED TO THE REST OF YOU HUMAN VERMIN, SHE'S QUITE INTELLIGENT.
...A CHARMING ONE.
NAMI WILL CONTINUE TO DRAW SEA CHARTS FOR ME IN THIS ROOM FOREVER.
...I'LL BUY HER ALL THE BEAUTIFUL CLOTHES SHE WANTS! SHE WILL WANT FOR NOTHING.
I'LL FEED HER...
AND ALL SHE HAS TO DO IS THE THING SHE LOVES BEST.
AFTER ALL...
... WE'RE SHIP-MATES.

WHAT'S GOING ON UP THERE!?
HEY!! WHAT HAPPENED TO LUFFY!?

WHAT !?
!!!

...!!?
BOOM
HEY !!!
WHAT'S THAT !!?
GASP!!
IT'S A DESK.
PHEW
IT'S JUST A DESK.
OH ...
NO WAY! I THOUGHT IT WAS ARLONG!
WHAT!? YOU THOUGHT THE SAME THING, JOHNNY!
OH!
GEEZ, PARTNER!! DON'T YOU HAVE ANY FAITH IN HIM!?
PHEW! I WAS AFRAID IT WAS LUFFY.
!

THWAK!!!
BLAST YOU!! WHAT ARE YOU DOING !!!?
BAM!!!
LUFFY ...?
KRASH!!
KRESH!!
KA
BAM!!!
THOOM!!

YOUR DESK! YOUR PENS!
THIS WILL BE YOUR ROOM FROM NOW ON!
EVERY-THING YOU NEED IS RIGHT HERE!!
WHAT'S THAT STUFF COMING DOWN?
BOOM...
KRASH!!
THUD THUD...
KRAK!
KROOSH!!!
THWOOSH!!!
CHUP
YOU LOUSY JERK !!!

BLAST!! MY CHARTS !!
FWUP
FWUP
!!
THUD THUD..
TUMB!
WA
MY SEA CHARTS !!!
UMF !!!
AND DON'T LEAVE THIS ROOM UNTIL YOU'RE DONE!! GOT THAT !!?
HERE'S THE NEW INFORMATION. NOW GET CRACKING ON THOSE CHARTS!!
TH UD
THUD
THUD..
KRASH!!
YOU DREW THIS CHART WRONG ON PURPOSE !!!
YOU NASTY GIRL! YOU CAN'T FOOL ME!!
KLONK!
UNH !!!

AGH !!
CURSE YOU! YOU'RE DESTROYING EIGHT YEARS OF NAMI'S WORK!!!
huff huff
WHAP!
BWAH HA HA HA HA !!
NOJIKO ...!!!
BELLE-MÈRE ...!!
KA-BOOM
THAT'S SOME FIGHT!
...
WHA
GAAGH !!!
!?
P!!!

...
THANK YOU.

...
KLAK KLAK KLAK
IT'S OVER.

WHAT IS IT!!? WHAT'S GOING ON!!?

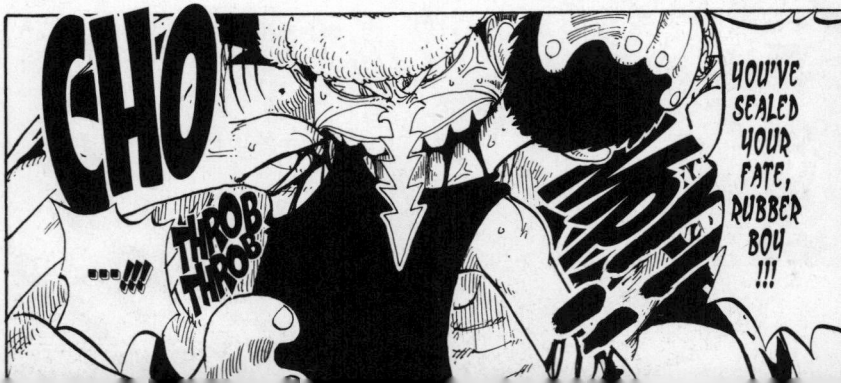
CHO
THROB THROB
...!!!
YOU'VE SEALED YOUR FATE, RUBBER BOY !!!

GAH!
I DON'T CARE HOW GREAT THE FISH-MEN ARE!!
!?
I DON'T CARE ABOUT SEA CHARTS OR ANY OF THAT !!!
WHAP!!
THAT STUFF DOESN'T MEAN ANYTHING TO ME!!!
BUT I'VE FINALLY FIGURED OUT HOW TO SAVE HER!!
KRAK
!!!!
AARGH !!!

GRRR..
THE PROBLEM IS THIS ROOM!!!
SHE HATED BEING STUCK HERE!! I'M GONNA SMASH IT TO SMITHEREENS !!!!
...!?
!!?
KRAKK
GUM-GUM ...

KRA
SH!!!
KRAK
KRAK!!
...CAN BRING DOWN ARLONG PARK !!!
GET AWAY FROM THOSE CHARTS!!! NO PUNY HUMAN...
WIP
WIP
WIP
!
GWAHH!
SHARK...
!?

...TOOTH DRILL !!!!
BAM!!!
WOOOOOOOO
...BATTLE AXE !!!!
REEEEEEE

!!!
CHO
NK
!!!
!!!?
TO
M
P
GRAAH
!!!!
GAAAH
!!!
KRK
KRK
KRK
KRK
KRK
KRK
KRKKRK
ARGH!

WOOOOOO
!!!
BOOM
BOOM
BOOM
BOOM
AARLONG PARK
AAAARGH!!!!
!?
...!!!
WHAT'S GOING ON!!!?

KRASH!!!
!!!!
WOO
WOOOOO
HUFF...
HUFF...
HUFF
HUFF
HUFF
!
SNAP!
HUFF
HUFF
BUT LUFFY'S STILL IN THERE !!!
NAMI!! C'MON!!
WATCH OUT, EVERY-BODY!! GET BACK !!!
WUZZ
WUZZ
IT'S GONNA COLLAPSE !!!
THIS IS CRAZY !!
LOOK!! THE SHOCK WAS TOO MUCH!! ARLONG PARK'S ...!!!
RRMMBB
RRMMBB
KREEK
WUZZ
WUZZ
KLAK
KLAK
KLUNK
HUH ?

LOOSIN
!!!!?
OMG
OMM!!!

KA-B
LUFFY !!!!
THO

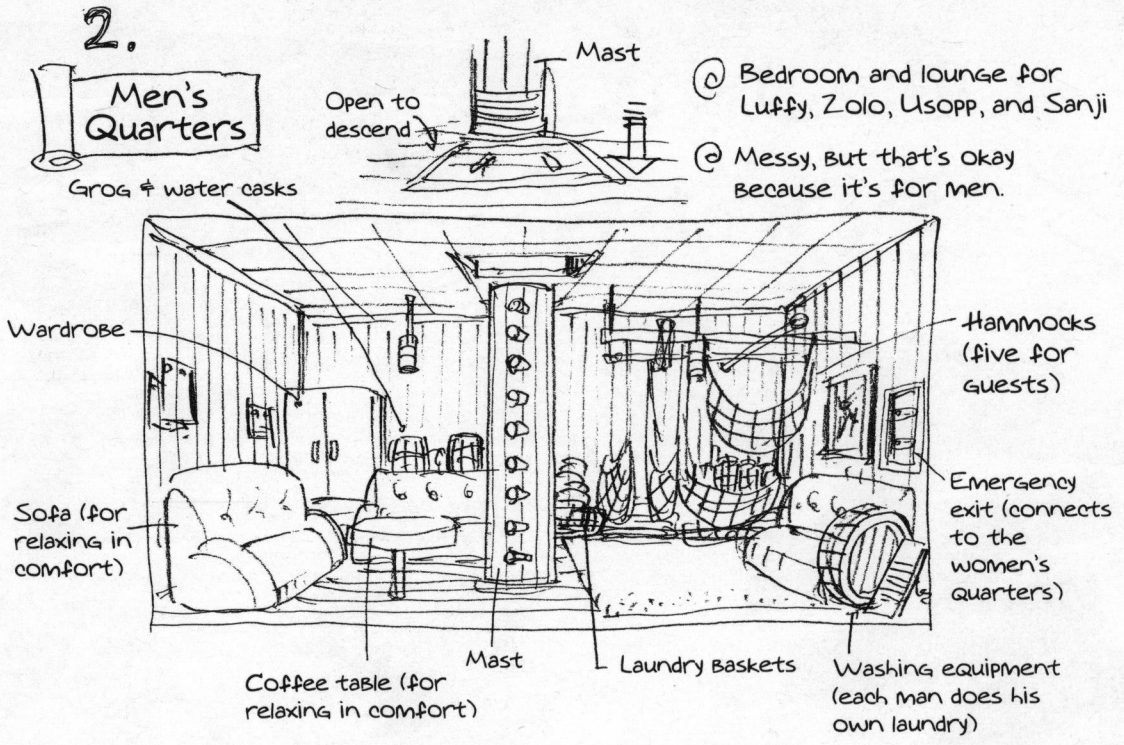
2.
Men's Quarters
Mast
Open to descend
@ Bedroom and lounge for Luffy, Zolo, Usopp, and Sanji
@ Messy, but that's okay because it's for men.
Grog & water casks
Wardrobe
Hammocks (five for guests)
Emergency exit (connects to the women's quarters)
Sofa (for relaxing in comfort)
Mast
Laundry baskets
Washing equipment (each man does his own laundry)
Coffee table (for relaxing in comfort)

Chapter 94: THE OTHER VILLAIN

RRMMMBB!!
WHAT'S GOING ON? WHAT'S ALL THE RACKET?
...
WOOOO
THUD!
UGH!
KLAK
KLAK...
SHORT
KOOK

WOOO!!
FISH FISH
1949

WHAT HAPPENED IN THERE!!?
PCE
WHOA ...!!
ARLONG PARK IS IN RUINS!!!

LUFFY ...

WITH EVERY-THING DE-STROYED, YOU DON'T THINK...?
WHO WON!!?

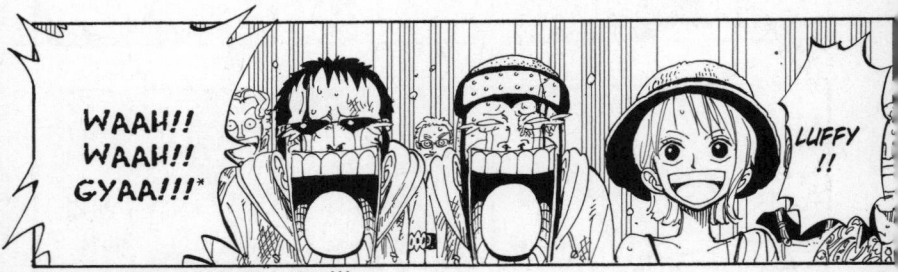

*TRANSLATION: BROTHER LUFFY!!!

PLUP...
PLUP...
IS HE ALL RIGHT?
HUFF...
NO!!!
NAMI!!!
...?

THOOM
YOU'RE ONE OF US NOW !!!!
DO
OM!!

UH-HUH !!!
PLIP!
...
MR. GENZO!!
WHUP
!!
TA-DAH
IT'S LIKE A DREAM. I NEVER THOUGHT I'D SEE THIS DAY.
HE DID IT, NOJIKO!! HE WON!! ♡
HE WON!!
HOORAY
ARLONG PARK HAS FALLEN !!!!

HEE HEE HEE !!

10

DA-DOOM!!!
HUIK HUIK HUIK HUIK !!!
!!?
HOLD EVERY-THING !!!

IT COULD'VE BEEN A FLUKE, BUT SOMEHOW YOU TWO-BIT PIRATES...
...DEFEATED THE FISH-MEN.
MARINE
IT'S MY LUCKY DAY!!!
I SAW THE WHOLE THING. WELL DONE.

HIM!!

DOOM!!!
THROW DOWN YOUR WEAPONS!!! YOUR VALIANT DEEDS...
...WILL GO ON THE RECORD OF CAPTAIN NEZUMI OF NAVY UNIT 16!!!
NOW, THANKS TO YOU, THE GOLD I WAS SUPPOSED TO GIVE TO ARLONG...
...AND ALL THE TREASURE IN ARLONG PARK, ARE MINE!!!
!!!?
KRUNCH
KRUNCH
KRUNCH
AAAAGH!!!
DON'T BE A WET BLANKET.
WE'RE CELEBRATING OUR VICTORY.
ZOLO!!

HE STILL DOESN'T GET IT.
SOB.
SOB.
YOU'D BETTER NOT MESS WITH ME. I'LL MAKE YOU REGRET IT.

...AND WRECKING BELLE-MÈRE'S TANGERINE GROVE.
THIS IS FOR SHOOTING NOJIKO...
HUH!?

PLOP!

!!!!?

SPLASH
CAPTAIN !!!

HIT HIM A THOUSAND TIMES MORE!!
THANK YOU, NAMI!
I FEEL BETTER NOW.

AND ONE MORE THING...
THAT MONEY BELONGS TO THE PEOPLE OF THIS ISLAND.
AND YOU DON'T GET ANY OF THE TREASURE OF ARLONG PARK!!
NOW YOU GUYS ARE GOING TO CLEAN UP THESE FISH-MEN... ...AND HELP REBUILD GOSA!!
TUNK TUNK TUNK
OW!! OW!! WHATEVER YOU SAY!!
SPLASH!!
GASP!!!

OKAY! OKAY!
YOU CAN HAVE IT!
MARINE
TUNK TUNK
VEEN
GIVE ME BACK MY MONEY!!!

REMEMBER THIS!!! YOU'VE INCURRED MY WRATH!!! NOW SOMETHING TERRIBLE WILL HAPPEN TO YOU!!!
SO YOU'RE THE CAPTAIN!!!
I'LL PAY YOU BACK IN SPADES !!!!
OOOO

I WON'T FORGET THIS, YOU ROTTEN PIRATES!!! YOU IN THE STRAW HAT!!! YOU SAID YOUR NAME WAS LUFFY!!!
VEEN!!

HEY, WHAT'LL WE DO IF SOMETHING TERRIBLE REALLY DOES HAPPEN!!?
THAT'S NOT IT, YOU IDIOT.
HOW DID HE KNOW ABOUT ME BECOMING KING OF THE PIRATES?
YOU MARK MY WORDS!!
splash
splash
splash
HE SAYS SOMETHING TERRIBLE'S GOING TO HAPPEN.
TUG
YOU NEVER KNOW...
KLIK
KLIK
KLIK
HMPH. WHO'D HAVE IMAGINED WE'D BE SAVED BY PIRATES?
LET'S TELL EVERYONE ON THE ISLAND THE GOOD NEWS!!!
YAHO
COME ON, EVERYONE!!! WE SHOULDN'T BE CELEBRATING ALL BY OURSELVES!!!
ARLONG PARK HAS BEEN DESTROYED !!!

IT'S ALL OVER, BELLE-MÈRE.
SPLOOSH
IT TOOK EIGHT YEARS, BUT FINALLY...
... EVERYBODY'S FREE!!

I'M SURE SHE WOULDN'T HAVE WANTED HER PRECIOUS DAUGHTER JOINING THOSE SEA-WOLVES.
OF COURSE NOT!!
?
WOULD YOU HAVE LISTENED IF SHE'D TRIED TO STOP YOU?

MR. GENZO, NOJIKO ...
HUH?
KLIK KLIK
IF BELLE-MÈRE WERE STILL ALIVE...
...DO YOU THINK SHE WOULD HAVE STOPPED ME FROM BECOMING A PIRATE?

BLEH !!!
ABSO-LUTELY NOT!!!

IT'S CRAZY THAT HE CAN EVEN MOVE.
YEAH, BUT IT'D TAKE A NORMAL PERSON TWO YEARS TO RECOVER...
THE IDIOT.
BLAB
BLAB
AAARRGH!!
THEY'RE STILL AT IT.
YACK
YACK
WHY A MUSICIAN?
...BUT A MUSICIAN SHOULD COME FIRST, RIGHT?
A DOCTOR? THAT WOULD BE NICE...
IS THERE A DOCTOR ON YOUR SHIP?
YOU NUMBSKULL! TRYING TO FIX SUCH A SERIOUS INJURY YOURSELF!!
OUCH...
WELL, PIRATES SING, DON'T THEY?
ZZZ
ZZZ
HA HA HA HA HA
... YOU'RE BELLE-MÈRE'S DAUGHTER, ALL RIGHT !!!
THERE'S NO DOUBT ABOUT IT...
WHY ARE YOU LAUGHING, MR. GENZO?
HA HA HA HA HA!!
HA HA HA...I CAN'T HELP IT!

HQ!!? THIS IS CAPTAIN NEZUMI, MC 00733 OF UNIT 16!!
HELLO! NAVY HQ!!
HELLO !?
NAVAL BASE UNIT 16
MARINE
16
I HAVE A REQUEST!!!
YOU DON'T HAVE TO SHOUT. I CAN HEAR YOU.
NAVY UNIT 16 TELESNAIL
...AND HIS FOUR HENCHMEN ...
SQU
AWK
DO YOU HEAR ME!? THE PIRATE LUFFY, WHO WEARS A STRAW HAT...
NAVY HQ TELESNAIL
NAVY HQ INFORMATION OFFICE
SKREEK
LUFFY AND...
SQUAWK
...SHOULD BE CONSIDERED ENEMIES OF THE STATE!!!

...WE MUST PUT A PRICE ON THEIR CAPTAIN'S HEAD!
YES, SIR!
WHAK!
CONSIDERING HOW DANGEROUS THESE MARAUDERS ARE...
I DID MY BEST.
COULDN'T YOU HAVE TAKEN A BETTER PICTURE?
AFTER CONFIRMING THE FACTS, I'LL REQUEST APPROVAL FROM THE GENERAL STAFF.
BLINK
MARINE
KLAK KLAK KLAK KLAK
SQUAWK
I'M SENDING YOU A PICTURE OF HIM!!!
DOOM!
KLAK KLAK
SEND OUT A WORLD-WIDE ALL-POINTS BULLETIN FOR HIS HEAD!!!!
WELL, GET THIS STRAIGHT!! HE'S A VICIOUS PIRATE!! I WANT HIM DEAD OR ALIVE!!!

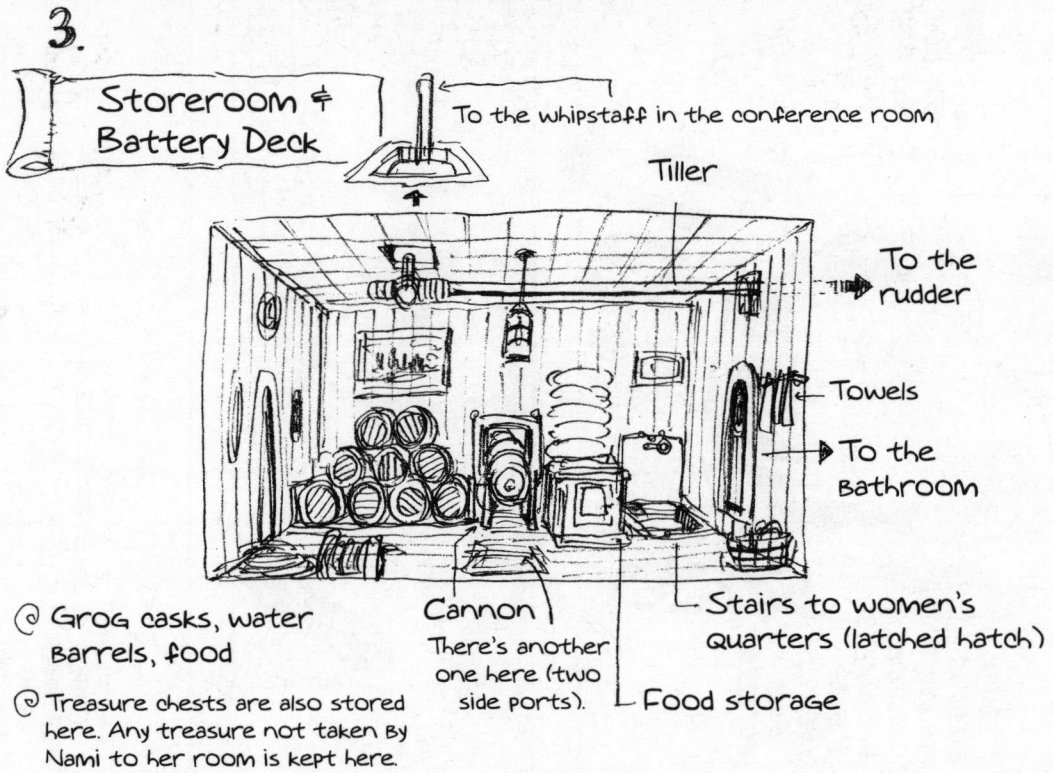
3.
Storeroom & Battery Deck
To the whipstaff in the conference room
Tiller
To the rudder
Towels
To the bathroom
Cannon
There's another one here (two side ports).
Stairs to women's quarters (latched hatch)
Food storage
Grog casks, water barrels, food
Treasure chests are also stored here. Any treasure not taken by Nami to her room is kept here.

Chapter 95: SPIN, PINWHEEL

NIGHT FELL AT LAST.
AHHAHAHAHA GAHAHAHA
SPLAP
THE SEA WAS CALM ONCE MORE.
AH HA HA HA HA HA HA HA HA
THE WHOLE ISLAND CELEBRATED THAT NIGHT...
...AND CONTINUED ON THROUGH THE FOLLOWING NIGHT.
EVERYONE WAS LIVING FOR THE MOMENT.
EVERYONE LIVED TO LAUGH.

WHAT'S WITH ALL THE MEAT?
HEY, SANJI!! THAT MELON YOU WERE EATING!! WAS THERE SOMETHING ON IT?
BOY, DID I EAT. SOMETIMES IT'S GOOD TO DO NOTHING BUT EAT.
BLAB
BLAB
MUNCH
MUNCH
MUNCH
MUNCH
YACK
YACK
OH!
THOOM!!

ALL HE DOES IS EAT.
I'LL GO LOOK AROUND !!
NOW, WHERE DID I GET IT...?
I DUNNO. THE PLACE IS ONE BIG PARTY.
GLUG
TMP TMP!!
I'VE HAD MY FILL OF FOOD.

WHERE'D YOU GET THAT!?
PRO-SCIUTTO AND MELON !!?
YEAH, IT WAS PROSCIUTTO... AND FRESH HAM.
Sounds good!!
FWIK

NOW I'M GONNA SING !!!
I'M CAPTAIN USOPP!!
DOOM!
AND THAT'S HOW I BROUGHT DOWN THE FISH-MEN!
GIMME YOUR AUTO-GRAPH!
HOORAY!
RAAA
AAA
AAA
tre FIGHTING!

NOW I'M GONNA FIND ME A GIRL!
HAHAHAHA
Hooray!
Wait for me!
HRONK ...

YOUR DAUGHTERS HAVE GROWN INTO WONDERFUL, STRONG YOUNG WOMEN...
BELLE-MÈRE...

GLUG GLUG
KLIK KLIK KLIK ...
...IS ALMOST LIKE SEEING YOU ALIVE AGAIN.
GLUG...

GLUG
GLUG
LOOKING AT THEM...

...MAKE THE MOST OF OUR LIVES.
FROM NOW ON...
... WE'RE GOING TO...

SO IT'S TIME FOR US...
...TO LIVE OUR LIVES TO THE FULLEST AND LAUGH LIKE FOOLS!!!
THERE HAVE BEEN SO MANY SACRI-FICES.

HOLD IT, KID!!!
I'M GOING BACK.
TMP TMP TMP

AW, THERE'S NO FOOD HERE.
HUH?
...

BA-BUMP!
PROSCIUTTO AND HAM!!!

YEAH, SOMEBODY DIED...
...A LONG TIME AGO.
GLUG
MUNCH
MUNCH
?
IT'S A GRAVE... DID SOMEBODY DIE?

YEAH, THOSE.
IT'S "CONDO-LENCES."
... COMBO-NINSES... HUH?
MY COMBO-LENCES...
ACCEPT MY CONGO-LESES...?
LISTEN, KID. NAMI'S GOING TO SAIL OFF WITH YOU PIRATES. IT WILL BE A DANGEROUS VOYAGE.

WELL, IN THAT CASE ...
...PLEASE ACCEPT MY CONGO-LENCES... HUH?

KLIK KLIK
KLIK...
BUT IF YOU GUYS DO ANYTHING TO MAKE HER UNHAPPY, I'LL KILL YOU!!!!
...
I WOULDN'T DO ANY--

I UNDERSTAND.
NOD

...

DO YOU UNDER-STAND !!!?

READ THIS WAY
I THOUGHT THAT AT FIRST.
...BECAUSE THIS DIDN'T HAPPEN IN TIME TO SAVE YOUR FATHER.
I THOUGHT YOU'D BE UPSET...
YACK YACK
WHADDAYA MEAN?
HMPH. YOU'RE NO FUN.
WHAT DID I DO!!?
OW! OW! WHY ARE YOU PINCHING ME!!?
CHEEKY BOY.
KRERK
ZING ZING
...REGRETS ARE A WASTE OF TIME.
THEN I REALIZED...
BEING A MEANIE'S FINE BY ME.
HA HA HA HA HA HA!!
YOU'RE DOING A GOOD JOB ALREADY!!
HMPH...
I WAS ALL SET TO PICK ON YOU AGAIN.
YACK
YOU TATTOOED MEANIE!!!
YACK

BA-BOOM BA-BOOM...
THAT'S HOW IT IS WITH TATTOOS.
NOT COM-PLETELY.
YOU'LL ALWAYS HAVE A SCAR.

BOOM BOOM
WILL IT BE COMPLETELY GONE?
WA HA HA
HA HA HA HA
BONG BONG

...

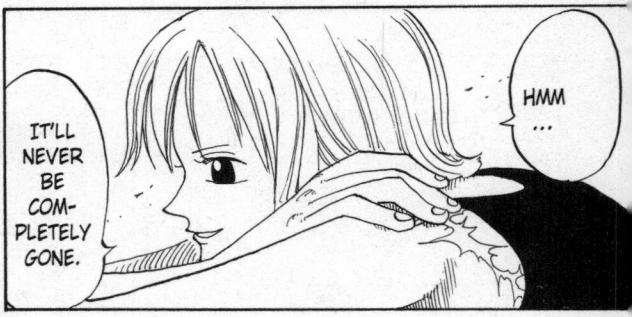
IT'LL NEVER BE COM-PLETELY GONE.
HMM ...

I'M NOT ONE OF THEM!! BUT NOW I'VE BEEN BRANDED A PIRATE!!!
I DON'T WANT ANYONE TO SEE MY TATTOO.

...

NAMI...

IT'S NOTHING. IT'S JUST A DECORATION.
SO WHAT?
NOJIKO!! YOU GOT A TATTOO!?

BUT...
HA HA HA HA HA!
I'M JUST LIKE YOU, NAMI.

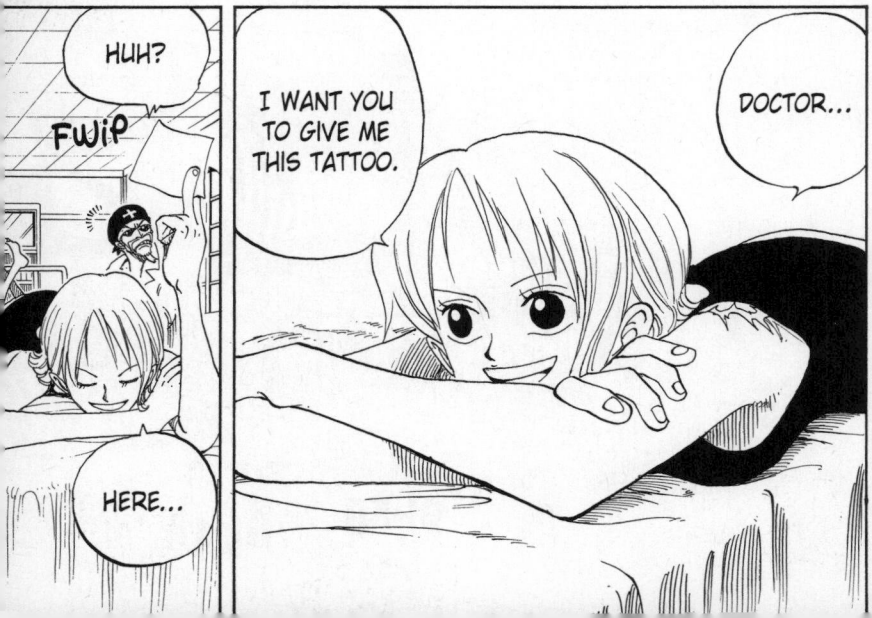
HUH?
FWIP
HERE...
I WANT YOU TO GIVE ME THIS TATTOO.
DOCTOR...

SONG NO. 6, "USOPP'S CHEER"!
WA HA HA HA
GA HA HA HA HA!!
HA HA HA HA
AH HA HA HA HA! THOSE TWO SURE CAN DANCE!

HA HA HA HA
WAAAAAAAA
HA HA HA HA

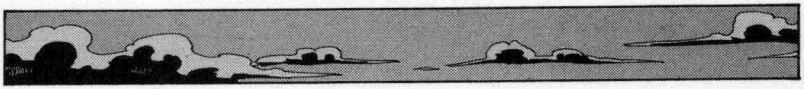

YACK YACK
THE MORNING OF DEPARTURE...
BLAB BLAB

DOOM!
WE'LL SAY GOODBYE HERE.
HOPE WE MEET AGAIN SOMEDAY.
WE'RE GOING BACK TO BEING BOUNTY HUNTERS.
THANKS FOR EVERYTHING, LUFFY.

YOU TOO.
OKAY. YOU GUYS TAKE CARE.

YOU!! THERE WASN'T ANY PROSCIUTTO ANYWHERE!!
DOOM
NAMI'S NOT COMING!!? WHY NOT!!?
MAYBE SHE'S NOT COMING.
HMM... SHE'S NOT HERE YET.

SHE SAYS IT'S OKAY.
SHE'LL JUST STEAL MORE.
YACK
BESIDES, SHE RISKED HER LIFE FOR IT...
SHE CAN'T TRAVEL WITHOUT MONEY!!
YACK
WHAT!?
SHE'S GOING TO LEAVE ALL THE MONEY!? ALL 100 MILLION BERRIES?

...WHO OWE HER!!
THAT FOOL. WE'RE THE ONES...
...ONCE HER MIND IS MADE UP, SHE WON'T BUDGE.
I TOLD HER TO TAKE AT LEAST A LITTLE MONEY, BUT...

TA-DOOM
HUH?
SET SAIL... NOW !!!!
NAMI!?

SHE SAID TO SET SAIL, SO LET'S DO IT.
SHE STARTED RUNNING. WHAT'S SHE UP TO!?
TO MP!!
...
!!?

FWAP
RAISE THE SAIL!!!
NO WAY!!
...WITHOUT GIVING US A CHANCE TO THANK HER!?
DON'T TELL ME SHE'S GOING TO LEAVE...
LET US THANK YOU PROP-ERLY!!!
STOP, NAMI!!!
TMP TMP TMP TMP TMP
...
WAIT, NAMI!!! YOU CAN'T JUST LEAVE US LIKE THIS!!!
FWOOM
GET MOV-ING !!
HEY, THEY'RE SAILING!!!
BUT WE WANTED TO THANK YOU GUYS ONE MORE TIME!!

SWIP
SWIP
SWIP
NAMI!!!

SHE SHOULD LEAVE THE WAY SHE WANTS.
ARE YOU SURE WE SHOULD LET HER DO THIS?

SHOOm ....!
NAMI !!!

TOMP!!

WHY!!?

HUH !?
!
MINE IS GONE TOO !!!
AND MINE !!
SO'S MINE !!
MINE TOO!
HEY!! MY WALLET'S GONE!!!
WAAAAAAH
KLUNK KLUNK
!!?
SWUP
KLUNK KLUNK...
TAKE CARE, EVERY-BODY. ♡
HEE !!

SHE TRICKED US!!!!
DOOM!!!
WHY YOU...
HA HA HA HA!!
WAY TO GO, NAMI!!
SHE COULD DOUBLE-CROSS US AGAIN.
SHE HASN'T CHANGED ONE BIT.
TROUBLE-MAKER!!!
HEH HEH...
GIVE US BACK OUR WALLETS!!!
COME BACK HERE!!!
YOU THIEV-ING CAT!!!
GRAAAAH

BELLE-MÈRE, I'M OFF...
SNIFF
WE'RE GRATEFUL TO YOU ALL!!!
RAAAAAH
TMP
TMP
TMP
COME BACK SOON !!!
TAKE CARE!!!
!
HEY, KID!! DON'T FORGET YOUR PROMISE!!!
DO OMF
I'LL BE BACK !!!!
BYE, EVERY-ONE !!!!

SHE GOT US!!

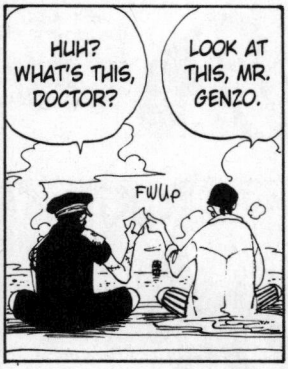
HUH? WHAT'S THIS, DOCTOR?
LOOK AT THIS, MR. GENZO.
FUUUP

HAVE FUN, NAMI.
HA HA
THAT SISTER OF MINE IS SOME-THING.

...AND A PINWHEEL, SHE SAID.
IT'S A TANGER-INE...

SHE HAD THIS TATTOO DONE.
WHAT IS THIS SYMBOL?

HEH HEH... I WON'T BE NEEDING IT ANYMORE.
HUH? MR. GENZO, WHERE'S YOUR PINWHEEL?

YOU MAKE HER CRY BECAUSE YOU LOOK SO SCARY.
I JUST WANT TO SEE HER SMILE.
WAAAAAAAH
B-BUT WHAT CAN I DO ABOUT IT?
NO, MR. GENZO!! DON'T COME NEAR NAM!!
WAAAH!!
HA HA HA HA HA HA!!
MR. GENZO, A PINWHEEL'S NOT GOING TO...
HEE HEE...
I'LL WEAR IT FROM NOW ON.
HOW'S THIS? THIS'LL MAKE HER LAUGH, WON'T IT!?
KLIK KLIK KLIK KLIK
TA-DAH
COME ON! LAUGH FOR ME, NAM!
HEY! SHE'S LAUGHING!!
THE SKIES ARE CLEAR AND THE WINDS ARE FAIR.
KLIK KLIK
KLIK KLIK...
AND THE PINWHEEL MERRILY SPINS.

4.

Women's Quarters

@ Nami's room. It's clean.

Chapter 96: THE MEANEST MAN IN THE EAST

KOBY AND HELMEPPO'S CHRONICLE OF TOIL
VOL. 12: "MORGAN RUNS"

YOU'RE CHARGING TOO MUCH!
DID YOU RAISE THE PRICE AGAIN?

WHAT'S A NEWSPAPER OR TWO?
IF YOU RAISE IT AGAIN, I'M NOT BUYING FROM YOU ANYMORE.
KAW
KLINK!
NEWS PAPER

STOP SQUAWKING!! I'M TRYING TO DEVELOP THE ULTIMATE KILLER, THE PEPPER SAUCE STAR!!
...IT'S TIME TO MAKE MONEY FOR MYSELF. I DON'T WANT TO BE A PENNILESS PIRATE.
DON'T BE STUPID! NOW THAT ARLONG'S GONE...
ANYONE WHO GETS THIS IN HIS EYES...

YOU'RE DONE COLLECTING MONEY, AREN'T YOU?
IF YOU READ ONE EVERY DAY, IT'S GOOD FOR THE BRAIN.
KAW

NO!!
WHAT? CAN'T I HAVE JUST ONE!?
GAAA-AGH!!!
FWOOSH
AARGH !!!
HANDS OFF!!!
...WON'T STAND A CHANCE!!
SPLASH!
KRASH!!
AW, THANK YOU, SANJI. ♡
NAMI, I SHALL GUARD THIS GROVE WITH ALL THE LOVE IN MY HEART!!
DOOM!!
THIS IS NAMI'S TANGERINE GROVE!! I WON'T LET YOU TOUCH THEM!!
FWUp!
OKAY. I'M IN TOO GOOD A MOOD TO FIGHT.
hee hee hee hee hee
THERE WAS ANOTHER COUP D'ÉTAT IN VIRA.
THE WORLD SURE IS IN TURMOIL.
FWUp!
YAY! WE'RE FINALLY SAILING FOR THE GRAND LINE!!
YEE-OWW!!
FWOOSH
SHE'S GOT HIM WRAPPED AROUND HER FINGER.

IT'S AN AD.
HUH?
HUH?
SWIP...

UH-OH.
ZZZ...
OH!
OH...
OH...

AND AT LONG LAST, THE MERRY GO SAILS FOR THE GRAND LINE.
AAAAAAAH!!!

PLUNK...!
WOO
NAVY HEADQUARTERS, UNDER DIRECT CONTROL OF THE WORLD GOVERNMENT
NAVY
DOOM!
...ARE UNABLE TO DEAL WITH THESE PIRATES?
SO YOU'RE SAYING THAT OUR BRANCH UNITS...
THAT IS CORRECT.

"SAW-TOOTH" ARLONG OF THE FISH-MAN PIRATES, 20 MILLION!!
DON KRIEG OF THE PIRATE ARMADA, 17 MILLION.
BUGGY THE CLOWN, 15 MILLION.
WANTED
DEAD OR ALIVE
ARLONG
$20,000,000—
MARINE
WANTED
DEAD OR ALIVE
KRIEG
$17,000,000—
MARINE
WANTED
DEAD OR ALIVE
BUGGY
$15,000,000—
MARINE

...HAVE NOW BEEN SMASHED.
...BUT EACH OF THESE PIRATES IS WORTH OVER 10 MILLION. THEIR PIRATE RINGS...
COMMANDER BRANDNEW
NAVY HEADQUARTERS
THE AVERAGE REWARD IN THE EAST BLUE IS 3 MILLION BERRIES...

WHAT!!
WANTED
WE MUST NIP THIS EVIL IN THE BUD BEFORE IT SPREADS!!!
STARTING A REWARD AT 30 MILLION IS UNPREC-EDENTED...
...BUT WE BELIEVE IT'S NECESSARY.
DEAD OR A
MONKEY·D
$30,000,000

READ THIS WAY
THIS IS THE STRONG-HOLD OF LIBERTY. IN THIS AGE OF PIRATES, NO WEAK-NESS IS PERMITTED HERE!!!
BOOM!
ANYONE WHO WANTS TO LEAVE IS FREE TO DO SO!!!
WE ARE JUSTICE !!!
WOOO...
IT'S NOT THE FAULT OF THE CITIZENS IF THEY FALL PREY TO CUT-THROATS!!
...IT'S UP TO US, THE NAVY, TO USE OUR MIGHT TO CRUSH THEM!!!
IF EVIL FORCES SAIL THE SEAS...

NAVY
IN THE NAME OF ABSOLUTE JUSTICE !!!!
正義
JUSTICE

YES, SIR !!!!
FWA
正義
正義
DO

DOOM!
HA HA HA
THEY SAY WE'RE WORTH 30 MILLION BERRIES!!
HA HA HA HA!! WE'RE WANTED DEAD OR ALIVE!!
WANTED
DEAD OR ALIVE
MONKEY·D·LUFFY

YOU'RE GRINNING LIKE AN IDIOT. IT'S NOTHING TO BRAG ABOUT.
LOOK!! I'M KNOWN ALL OVER THE WORLD!!
AT THAT PRICE, HEADQUARTERS IS PROBABLY INVOLVED. THE TOUGHEST BOUNTY HUNTERS ARE GOING TO COME AFTER YOU, TOO.
THE NAVY'S HUNTING YOU, LUFFY!!
AS USUAL, YOU GUYS HAVE NO IDEA HOW SERIOUS THIS IS.
HA HA HA HA HA HA!!
SWU-MP
WANTED
DEAD OR ALIVE
MONKEY·D·LUFFY
DON'T BE JEALOUS! IF YOU GET TO BE A BIG SHOT, THEY MIGHT PUT YOU ON A POSTER TOO, EVEN IF YOU AREN'T A CAPTAIN.

HEY, THERE'S AN ISLAND.

YEAH!!
OKAY, LET'S SAIL FOR THE GRAND LINE, MEN!!
THIS IS NO TIME TO BE RELAXING IN THE EAST BLUE.

IF WE SEE THAT ISLAND...
THERE IT IS.
...THEN WE'RE APPROACHING THE GRAND LINE.
THE PIRATE KING, GOLD ROGER, WAS BORN THERE...
THAT'S WHERE THE FAMOUS ROGUETOWN IS.
...AND EXECUTED THERE.
THEY CALL IT "THE TOWN OF THE BEGINNING AND THE END."
WANT TO GO THERE?
IT'S WHERE THE PIRATE KING DIED!

DOON
ROGUE-TOWN TOWN OF THE BEGINNING AND THE END
Roguetown
YACK YACK
BLA B BLA B
SO THIS IS WHERE THE AGE OF PIRATES BEGAN.
WOW!! THIS PLACE IS HUGE!!

I GUESS I'LL FIND US SOME EQUIPMENT.
I CAN PROBABLY GET SOME GOOD COOKING INGREDIENTS HERE.
And some cute chicks.
TMP TMP
RIGHT!! I'M GOING TO GO SEE THE EXECUTION SCAFFOLD !!

I'LL BE GLAD TO LEND YOU SOME MONEY... AT 300% INTEREST.
HÉH HÉH
THERE'S SOMETHING I WANT TO BUY TOO.

OUR BOSS IS IN JAIL, THANKS TO YOU LOT. NOW YOU'RE GOING TO PAY.
SO...YOU'RE NOT WITH THAT MONSTER TODAY, EH!?
SHOPPING H
YACK YACK
BLAB BLAB BLAB
!
WELL, I'LL BE HAPPY TO TAKE YOU ON.
SCELTI
THEN YOU HAVEN'T HAD ENOUGH.
WOOO——...O
ALL RIGHT, THEN!!
WHAT!? YOU WANT TO FIGHT US!!?

...THAT BECAUSE OF HIM, OUR DREAMS OF ENTERING THE GRAND LINE ARE RUINED!!!
DIE! AND LET THAT MON-STER KNOW ...
HUH?
WHP..
!! WO OOO !!
!!?

!
FWUMP!!
OUCH!
KLAK
OH...
OH...
AH...
TUNK
ARE THESE YOURS ?
HEY.
OH.
FWEET FWEET
YOU SURE ARE STRONG, SISTER!!
YAY
KLAP KLAP
BLUSH
OH! HUH?
YAY
KLAP KLAP
AH HA HA HA HA!!
!!!
TH-THANK YOU VERY MUCH.
S-SORRY.

ON A CERTAIN ISLAND ...
AARGH !!
HAWK-EYE!!! NO!! WHAT ARE YOU DOING HERE!!?

DON'T GET EXCITED. I'M NOT HERE BECAUSE OF YOU.
WHERE'S YOUR CAPTAIN?

B...
B...
B...
BOSS!!!
TMP TMP TMP TMP TMP TMP TMP

CAMPING ON THIS ISLAND? HOW CARELESS.

DO OM!!!
HUH?

HUMPH. I DON'T CHALLENGE ONE-ARMED HAS-BEENS.
GRRR...
I'M IN A BAD MOOD. YOU HERE TO CHALLENGE ME?
GRRR...
HAWK-EYE. THIS IS UNEX-PECTED.

WHAT!!? NO WAY!!!
KLANK...!!
ABOUT A BOY IN SOME LITTLE VILLAGE...
...
HE REMINDED ME OF A STORY YOU TOLD ME LONG AGO.
I'VE FOUND AN INTERESTING PIRATE.
rustle
rustle

DOON!

SO, YOU'RE HERE...

...LUFFY.

"RED-HAIRED" SHANKS
PIRATE CAPTAIN

GOOD FOR HIM!
THIS VILLAGE MAY END UP BEING THE HOME OF A FAMOUS PIRATE YET!
THAT WOULD BE GREAT!!!
YACK YACK
HEY, LUFFY'S BECOME A WANTED MAN.
WINDMILL VILLAGE (LUFFY'S HOME-TOWN)
BLAB BLAB
ARE YOU WOR-RIED?
BUT IT WAS HIS DREAM.
A PIRATE'S A PIRATE!!
HEH HEH... LOOK HOW HAPPY LUFFY IS, MR. MAYOR.
Ye
ah!!
KLUNK...
Party time!
SHUT UP, FOOL!! WHAT'S SO GREAT ABOUT HAVING THIS VILLAGE BE HOME TO A CRIMINAL!?
GRRR GRRR GRRR
IT'S THE MAYOR!!
...OR HIS DESTINY...
HIS DREAM ...

5.

Gun Deck & Anchor Rope Storage

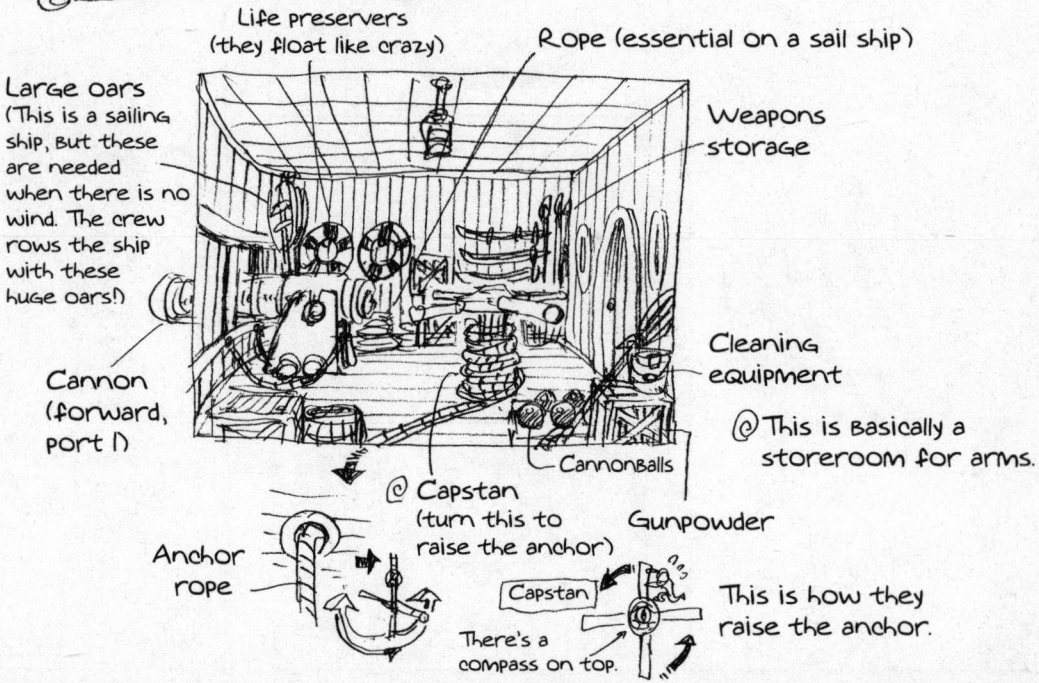

Chapter 97: KITETSU III

AND THIS?
VA-
VOOM
WHY, MADAM !!
OHH! SO ELEGANT !!

HOW'S THIS?
VA-
VOOM!
OH MY!! YOU LOOK STUNNING !!

SEXY!!
AND THIS?
EXQUI-SITE!!
AND THIS?
ELECTRIC!!
HOW'S THIS?
SO ELEMEN-TAL, MADAM!!
THIS?
ECCENTRIC !!
GLOVE FACTORY
ROBECCA

THEY'RE MUCH MORE COMFORT-ABLE.
MAYBE NEXT TIME!
I LIKE CASUAL CLOTHES.
I'll try somewhere else...
HUFF HUFF
GOOS GOOS GOOS GOOS

NO THANKS.
FOOMF
SO YOU'LL BE PURCHASING THEM ALL, I TAKE IT!?
HUFF HUFF
HEE!
HEE!
HUFF

DOOM!!
THE EXECUTION SCAFFOLD ...
YACK YACK
BLAB BLAB
THAT'S WHERE GOLD ROGER ...
BLAB BLAB
...WAS EXECUTED.
YACK YACK
THAT'S IT.
...DIED RIGHT THERE.
BLAB BLAB
YACK YACK
THE GREATEST PIRATE OF ALL TIME...

THIS IS WHERE ...
...THE GREAT AGE OF PIRATES BEGAN.

DO OM!
I WAS SO WEAK.
DARN IT!

YACK YACK
I DOUBT I'LL SEE HER AGAIN, THOUGH.
I GUESS FEMALE SWORDSMEN DO EXIST.
BLAB BLAB
STILL, I WAS WEAK.

I-I'M SORRY.
STILL...
AND SHE'S EVEN A SWORDS-MAN!
Like two peas in a pod.
IT'S UNCANNY HOW MUCH SHE LOOKS LIKE KUINA.

I WANT A SWORD.
AT A WEAP-ONS SHOP ...
ARMS SHOP
OH YES! YES, YES, YES, YES!
OLD SWORDS, NEWER SWORDS, AND BRAND-NEW SWORDS. WE HAVE 'EM ALL...
...AND A SOLID REPUTATION OF OVER 200 YEARS IN THE BUSINESS!
TA-DAH
hee hee hee
swup swup
MATSU WEAPONS SHOP OWNER
YES, YES. WELCOME!
PLEASE COME IN AND LOOK AROUND.
YOU'LL ONLY GET A BLUNT SWORD FOR 50,000...
... GOT IT!?
WHAT AN AMA-TEUR.
HM
PH!
SWUMP
TWO SWORDS FOR 100,000 BERRIES !?
THIS GUY'S A BUM.
SELL ME TWO SWORDS.
I HAVE 100,000 BERRIES.
100,000 ?

THE SWORD AT HIS WAIST... COULD IT BE...!!?

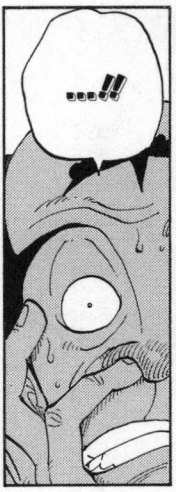
...!!

I'LL TAKE WHATEVER YOU'VE GOT. I'M LOW ON CASH RIGHT NOW.
!

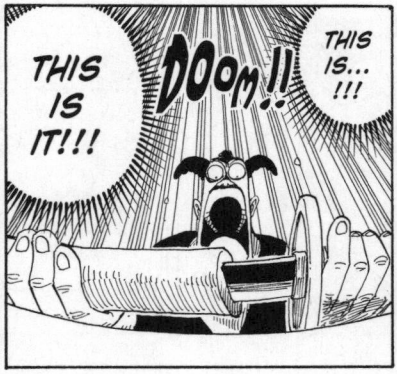
THIS IS IT!!!
DOOM!!
THIS IS... !!!

WHY ARE YOU SHAKING?
?
COULD I... HAVE A LOOK AT THAT SWORD?
ER...AH... COULD...
ACT NATURAL, ACT NATURAL ...

WHAT?
THIS SWORD'S NO GOOD.
SWUP!!
WAIT! SORRY, I LIED.

THIS POOR SUCKER WALKED IN WITH A LEGENDARY SWORD! JUST TALK TO HIM CALMLY...!!
CALM DOWN!! THIS IS YOUR BIG CHANCE !!

READ THIS WAY
HUH? WHAT ARE YOU TALKING ABOUT?
ER.. FORGET THAT.
500,000 BERRIES THEN!!!
I'LL GIVE YOU 200,000 BERRIES FOR IT.
THEN YOU'LL HAVE 300,000 AND YOU CAN BUY THREE SWORDS FOR 100,000 BERRIES EACH!
LOOK HERE, FRIEND. MAYBE WE CAN WORK AROUND YOUR LACK OF FUNDS.
THIS SWORD IS NOTHING SPECIAL, BUT IT MIGHT BE WORTH SOMETHING.
LISTEN ...
...THIS SWORD ISN'T FOR SALE AT ANY PRICE.
HOW CAN HE REFUSE !!?
I'LL GIVE YOU 650,000 BERRIES FOR IT!
GAAAH
WHAT THE HECK !?
I ALMOST HAVE HIM!
DON'T SAY IT!! DON'T SAY IT!!!
WHAT'S SHE DOING HERE!?
COULD IT BE...!!?
GULP!
WHOA !!! THAT SWORD !!!
!

THIS IS...
...THE WADO ICHIMONJI, THE STRAIGHT ROAD OF PEACE!!

LOOK AT THIS BLADE!
SURE, THAT'S ITS NAME...BUT IT'S NO GREAT SHAKES.

!?
"WADO" WHAT !?

JUST LOOK RIGHT HERE! THIS SWORD'S WORTH 10 MILLION BERRIES!!
TH ROB!
THROB!!
THROB!!!
"NO GREAT SHAKES"!? ARE YOU NUTS!? THIS IS ONE OF THE GREAT 21!! IT'S A FAMOUS SWORD!!

YOU'RE HERE TO PICK UP AUTUMN RAIN RIGHT!? I'VE POLISHED IT!!
EEK!
WHOA!
OH!
WHUP
WHAT'S A NOVICE LIKE YOU DOING WITH A FAMOUS SWORD, ANYWAY?
DAMAGING YOUR BUSINESS!? I'M SORRY! DID I SAY SOMETHING WRONG!?
WHY, YOU... I'LL SUE YOU FOR DAMAGING MY BUSINESS!!!
YOU IDIOT! WHY'D YOU HAVE TO TELL HIM THAT!!?
WHAM!!
I'VE NEVER SEEN SUCH A BEAUTIFUL SWORD! I COULDN'T HELP MYSELF!!
BUT SHE'S RIGHT. THAT SWORD IS WASTED ON SOMEONE LIKE YOU WHO DOESN'T KNOW ITS VALUE.
THAT IDIOT GIRL SAVED YOU.
IT IS A FAMOUS SWORD!!
FWIP!!
WHAT ARE YOU DOING!!?
KLAK KLAK KRASH!!
AAAH!!
LEAVE THAT SWORD AND GET OUT!!
I MET YOU ON THE STREET EARLIER!
HUH!?
PICK TWO.
THERE ARE SWORDS WORTH 50,000 BERRIES IN THAT BARREL.
WHAT'S HE SO MAD ABOUT?

BOUNTY HUNTER?
HAVEN'T YOU HEARD OF HIM? HIS NAME'S RORONOA ZOLO.

THREE SWORDS AT ONCE, HUH? JUST LIKE THAT BOUNTY HUNTER!
YOU MUST LIKE SWORDS!

THAT'S UNFOR-GIVABLE !!
USING A SWORD TO MAKE MONEY...
BUT IT'S AN EVIL NAME!!
THAT'S THE NAME OF A MASTER SWORDSMAN WHO'S FAMOUS THROUGHOUT THE EAST BLUE.
I KNOW THE NAME WELL.
KLAK
KLAK

AND MOST OF THE WORLD-FAMOUS SWORDS ARE IN THEIR HANDS.
ALL THE FAMOUS SWORDSMEN ARE EITHER PIRATES OR BOUNTY HUNTERS.
WHY IS THERE SO MUCH EVIL IN THE WORLD TODAY!?
THOSE SWORDS MUST BE CRYING.

THEN THAT MONSTER TOOK OVER THIS TOWN.
AND WHAT HAPPENED? THE CUSTOMERS STOPPED COMING.
I LIKE BAD GUYS!
THIS SHOP USED TO BE FILLED WITH MEN WHO WANTED TO SAIL THE GRAND LINE.
WELL, THERE ARE PROBABLY GOOD REASONS FOR THAT.
A MAN'S GOT TO DO WHAT HE CAN TO EAT IN THESE HARD TIMES.
DEVIL FRUIT!?
HE'S GOT THE POWER OF THE DEVIL FRUIT!!
KLAK
KLAK...
CAPTAIN SMOKER IS NOT A MONSTER !!
THEN I'M GOING TO COLLECT ALL THE FAMOUS SWORDS THAT HAVE FALLEN INTO THE HANDS OF THE EVIL MEN OF THE WORLD.
I'LL GET THE 12 SUPREME GRADE SWORDS, THE 21 EXCELLENT GRADE SWORDS AND THE 40 FINE GRADE SWORDS...EVEN IF IT KILLS ME!!
DOOM!
IN ANY CASE, I'LL USE MY AUTUMN RAIN...
...TO HONE MY SKILLS AS A SWORDS-MAN!

*ALSO KNOWN AS KITETSU THE THIRD.

THIS SWORD'S PREDECESSOR, KITETSU II, WAS AN EXCELLENT-GRADE SWORD!
IT'S WORTH A MILLION BERRIES!
WOW!! THIS IS A GENUINE FINE-GRADE SWORD!!
AND THE ORIGINAL KITETSU WAS A SUPREME-GRADE SWORD!!!
ER... YEAH.
...WERE 50,000 BERRIES EACH, RIGHT!?
HEY, MISTER, YOU SAID THESE SWORDS...
WOOOOOOO
THIS SWORD'S BE-WITCHED.
HUH? WHY NOT?
NO! NOT THAT ONE! I CAN'T SELL THAT ONE!!
THE FIRST KITETSU AND ITS SUCCESSORS ARE GOOD BLADES, BUT THEY'RE ALL CURSED!!
...!! WELL, YOU'RE RIGHT.
I CAN JUST TELL.
NO.
YOU'VE HEARD OF IT!?
!?

THESE DAYS, NO SWORDSMAN IN THE WORLD USES A KITETSU...
...AND IF HE DID, HE WOULDN'T BE AROUND LONG.
FAMOUS SWORDSMEN HAVE DIED TRAGIC DEATHS BECAUSE THEY WIELDED THE KITETSU SWORDS.

...AN EXPERT, EH!?
HAH! THOUGHT YOU WERE...
SHOW OFF!!

AND I WAS SO PUSHY.
I DIDN'T KNOW IT WAS SO DANGER-OUS!!
... FOR-GIVE ME!!
PLEASE ...

...BUT I MIGHT BE CURSED FOR IT.
I'D LIKE TO GET RID OF THAT SWORD MYSELF...

ARE YOU A FOOL? I CAN'T SELL YOU THAT SWORD!! IF YOU DIED, IT'D BE LIKE I KILLED YOU MYSELF!!

I'LL TAKE IT!!
I LIKE THIS SWORD !!

...VERSUS THIS SWORD'S CURSE.
WHY DON'T WE FIND OUT WHICH IS STRONGER?
HOW 'BOUT THIS THEN?
MY LUCK...
YOU'RE THE FOOL! JUST GET RID OF THAT THING!!
WHAK!!
AAGH! HONEY BUN...
...AM I!!?
FWIP
FWIP
FWIP...
IF I LOSE...
FWIP!
!?
...THEN I'M NOT MAN ENOUGH TO POSSESS IT...
OH !!!!
THAT BLADE'S RAZOR SHARP !!!
STOP FOOLING AROUND!! YOU'LL LOSE YOUR ARM!!!

KL
ANG!!

SWU
SH

OOOOOO

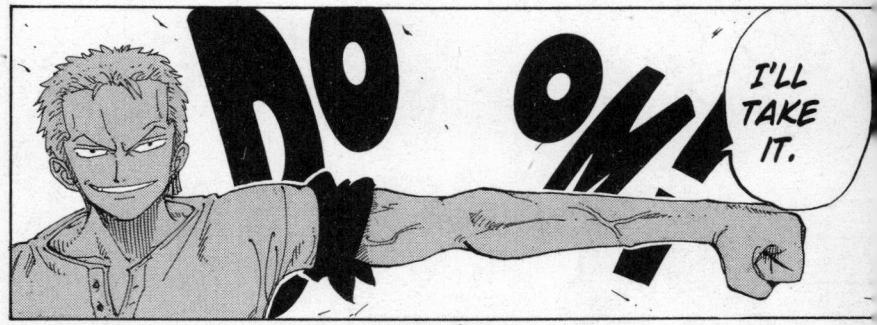
NO
OW!
I'LL TAKE IT.

HEY, WILL YOU CHOOSE ANOTHER ONE FOR ME?
SWUP...
WOW...!
FW
UMP!!!

*A SWORD TERM FOR AN IRREGULAR PATTERN.

MADOV
GLOVE FACTO
VILLA MEDICI
OTTINO
...MAKES ME FEEL WHOLE AGAIN.
AHH, HAVING THREE SWORDS ...

WOMEN DON'T UNDERSTAND ANYTHING!!
WELL, WELL. IMAGINE A MISER LIKE YOU GIVING AWAY YOUR SHOP'S TREASURES.

I- I CAN'T GET UP.

YES, DEAR !!!
GO CLEAN THE BATHROOM!!

WHAT'S WRONG WITH A MAN ENTRUSTING ANOTHER MAN WITH HIS DREAMS!!?

WE GOT A TIP ABOUT SOME PIRATES.
GO GET HER!!
AND HOW LONG'S THAT SUPPOSED TO TAKE!!?
SERGEANT TASHIGI WENT TO PICK UP A SWORD FROM THE SWORD SHOP.
WANTED
ISN'T TASHIGI BACK YET!!?
ROGUE-TOWN NAVAL BASE, MAIN GATE
THAT WOMAN IS INSUFFER-ABLE!
SHE'S AN EMBAR-RASSMENT TO THE NAVY!
SHOOM
DOOM!!
AYE-AYE, CAPTAIN SMOKER!!
I'VE GOT TO ADMIT, BIG CITIES HAVE A LOT GOING FOR THEM!!
FWOOO!
WHOO!!
YACK YACK
BLAB
BLAB
WOW...
WHAT A BEAUTY! ♡

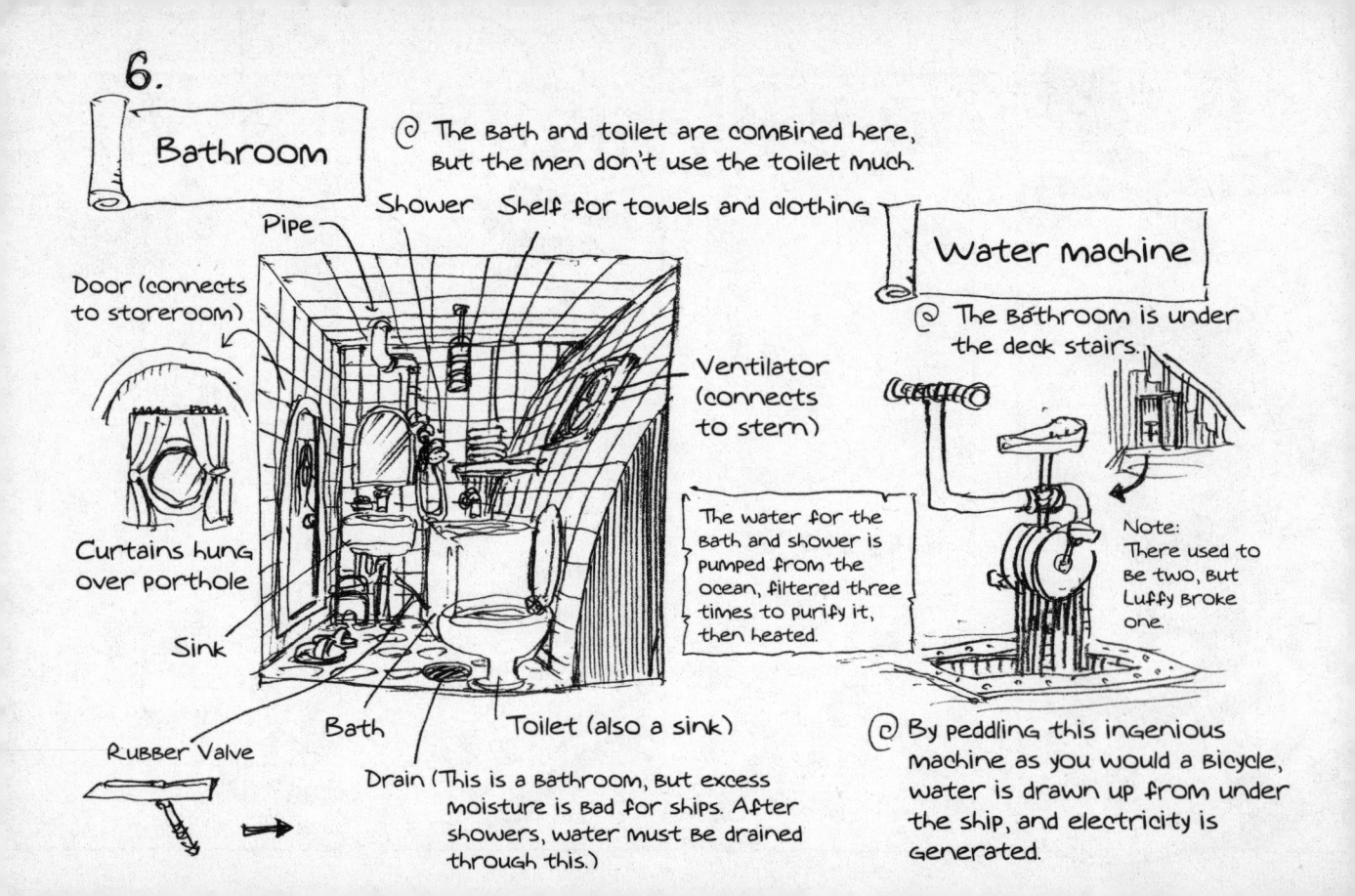
6.
Bathroom
The bath and toilet are combined here, but the men don't use the toilet much.
Shower
Shelf for towels and clothing
Pipe
Door (connects to storeroom)
Ventilator (connects to stern)
Curtains hung over porthole
Sink
Bath
Toilet (also a sink)
Rubber Valve
Drain (This is a bathroom, but excess moisture is bad for ships. After showers, water must be drained through this.)
The water for the bath and shower is pumped from the ocean, filtered three times to purify it, then heated.
Water machine
The bathroom is under the deck stairs.
Note: There used to be two, but Luffy broke one.
By peddling this ingenious machine as you would a bicycle, water is drawn up from under the ship, and electricity is generated.

Chapter 98: DARK CLOUDS

KOBY AND HELMEPPO'S CHRONICLE OF TOIL
VOL. 14: "A HINDRANCE TO THE ARTILLERY ATTACK"

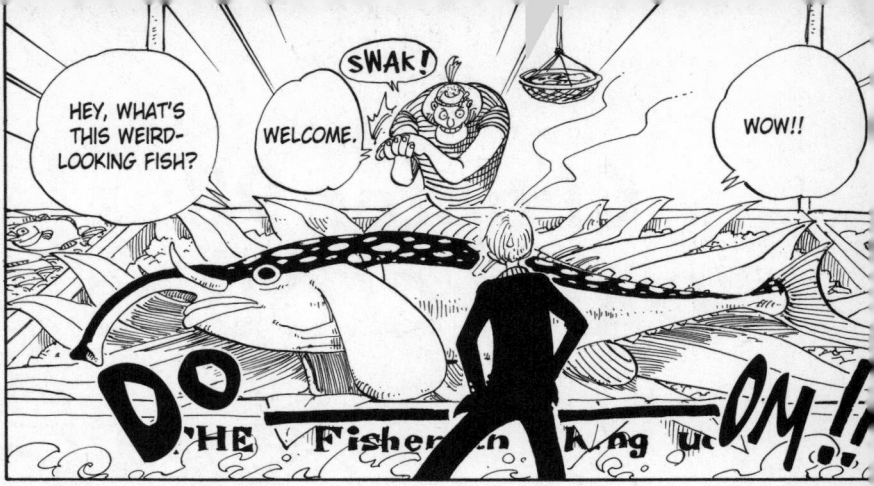
HEY, WHAT'S THIS WEIRD-LOOKING FISH?
WELCOME.
SWAK!
WOW!!

I'LL TAKE IT WHOLE.
NO.
throb
throb

YOU CAUGHT IT!?
I CAUGHT IT MYSELF !!
NEVER SEEN ONE IN THESE WATERS, HAVE YOU? IT SWAM IN FROM THE SOUTH SEAS.
THIS IS AN ELEPHANT TRUE BLUEFIN.
Did you really!?
SWAK!!
WANT ME TO SLICE IT UP?

WHAT ARE YOU, A HOUSE-WIFE?
WOW!!! THESE EGGS ARE CHEAP!!
But there's a one-per-customer limit.

WHAT'S HE DOING IN A SUPERMARKET ?
TMP TMP

IT'S TOO BAD ABOUT THAT LADY. SHE WAS A REAL BEAUTY, BUT I LOST SIGHT OF HER.
HEY, YOU'RE A BIG SPENDER.
TMP
TMP
HUH?
THE
Fisher

FUU MP!
ALL OF THEM!
I'LL TAKE ...
THESE!

?
COME AGAIN.
WIP WIP WIP
FUNK

HOW RUDE. OF COURSE I DO.
I HOPE YOU HAVE ENOUGH MONEY.
ALL OF THEM!?
FUNK

DO YOU HAVE A SHEET OF PLASTIC ?
EXCUSE ME, MA'AM.
PLASTIC? BUT THE WEATHER'S FINE.

THERE'S A STORM COMING.
THE BAROMETRIC PRESSURE HAS DROPPED.
AW, I WANTED TO STROLL AROUND A BIT LONGER.

THE AIR'S DIFFERENT.
BLAB BLAB
YACK YACK

WOW!
WHOA!
DOOM!!
YACK YACK
SO THIS IS WHAT THE KING OF THE PIRATES SAW...
BLAB BLAB
...JUST BEFORE HE DIED!!!
HEY, YOU!!! GET DOWN FROM THERE IMMEDIATELY!!

DOOM!!
WHY?
THAT'S THE SPECIAL EXECUTION SCAFFOLD! IT'S UNDER THE JURISDICTION OF THE WORLD GOVERNMENT!!!
KRU
NCH!
!?
COME DOWN RIGHT--
WAAAAAH!!
!!!
I'VE FOUND YOU AT LAST, LUFFY!! IT'S BEEN A LONG TIME!!
!
AAAAH
GASP
WUMP...
HEY, DON'T BE SO MEAN...
...MR. POLICE-MAN.

... FORGOTTEN THIS FACE?
SURELY, YOU HAVEN'T...
A PARAGON OF LOVELINESS !!!
BA-DOOM!
WHAT A BEAUTY!!
SHE'S GOR-GEOUS! ♡
WOO
AAAH
GASP
I DON'T KNOW YOU, BEAUTIFUL LADY.
?
DOOOOM!
WHO ARE YOU?

YES, AND I REALLY FELT IT.
...!!?
I HIT YOU!?
WHAT!?
WELL, I'LL NEVER FORGET YOU. YOU WERE THE FIRST MAN WHO EVER HIT MY LOVELY FACE.
throb throb
BA-BUMP!
TCHING...
IT WAS SO HARD.
AND I DO LOVE STRONG MEN.
THERE ISN'T A MAN IN THIS WORLD WHO WOULDN'T GROVEL AT MY FEET.
YES, I AM.
YOU'RE GOING TO BE MINE, LUFFY. ♡
YOU ARE! ♡
...WHO IS THE MOST BEAUTIFUL WOMAN ON THE SEAS!?
NOW TELL ME...

WHO ARE YOU?
YOU STILL DON'T KNOW!?
NO WAY!
SHUT UP!
SO WHAT!? ARREST HER!!
A-ASSISTANT INSPECTOR!! THIS IS DIFFICULT!! SHE'S SO BEAUTIFUL!!
SHAKE SHAKE
AND YOU!! GET OFF THE SCAFFOLD!!
THIS IS THE POLICE!! YOU THERE, WOMAN!! SURRENDER, OR ELSE!!!
WHAT? YOU'RE GOING TO ARREST ME?
YOU'RE UNDER ARREST FOR ASSAULTING A POLICE INSPECTOR!!!
KA-BAM!!
WAAH !!!
A TERRORIST BOMB!!!
DIE LAVISHLY!!!

THAT CHUNK OF FOUNTAIN IS HEADING STRAIGHT FOR HER!!!
!
WOOO!!!
OH NO!! SHE'S DOOMED !!!
SHOOM!!!
!!!?

...WHAT WAS THAT?
HEY! LOOK OUT!
WHAT HAPPENED!!? THE FOUNTAIN WENT RIGHT PAST HER!!
GASP

...CAN NEVER BE MARRED. YOU NEEDN'T WORRY.
WOOOOO
PARDON THE SPECTACLE, BUT HER SMOOTH, SILKY SKIN...

DOOM!
I AM THE EXQUISITE LADY ALVIDA!!

YOU LOOK KINDA DIFFERENT...
REALLY?

ALVIDA!? WHERE IS SHE!?
RIGHT HERE!! IT'S ME!!
YOU SILLY FOOL !!

I PARTOOK OF THE SLIP-SLIP FRUIT!!
NOW MY BEAUTIFUL SKIN CANNOT BE MARRED BY ANY ATTACK!!!
FW
Up
HEH HEH! NICE OF YOU TO NOTICE!
I ATE THE DEVIL FRUIT AND TRANSFORMED !!!

...WAS BARELY ENHANCED. HOWEVER, AS YOU SAID...
EEK
EEK
SADLY, MY BEAUTY ...

WE TEAMED UP IN ORDER TO FIND YOU.
...THERE'S SOMEONE YOU MUST DEFEAT FIRST!!
BUT IF YOU'RE GOING TO BECOME MY MAN...
AND HERE HE IS!!!

I DON'T THINK THAT'S IT.
...I DO LOOK A BIT DIFFERENT!! MY FRECKLES ARE GONE!!
KLAP KLAP!!

...I'VE DREAMED OF NOTHING BUT KILLING YOU. THAT'S WHAT GAVE ME THE STRENGTH TO MAKE IT BACK TO MY CREW.
SINCE THE DAY YOU DEFEATED ME...
WHAT'RE YOU MAKING ME SAY!!?
THERE WAS LAUGHTER, THERE WERE TEARS!! THERE WAS FRIENDSHIP AS WELL!!! BUT BUGGY PERSEVERED AND...
AND IT WAS AN EPIC ADVENTURE!! ESPECIALLY SINCE I WAS MISSING SOME BODY PARTS!!
WHY, YOU!!! YOU WON'T BE SO INSOLENT WHEN I'M DONE WITH YOU!!!
THOOM!!
OH, IT'S YOU, BUGGY.

AAAAAH
FREEZE, LAND-LUBBERS !!!
IT'S BUGGY THE CLOWN!!
KLIK !!!
YOU'RE ABOUT TO SEE JUST HOW TERRIFYING I CAN BE!!!
PIRATES !!!
!!?
VE EN!
WHA--
WELL DONE, CABAJI!!
HEY!!
IT'S BEEN A LONG TIME, EH, RUBBER MAN?
HOW'S RORONOA ZOLO?
WHUMP!!
UGH !!?
ARG !!
DOOM!
BWAH HA HA! WHAT AN HONOR!! YOU'RE GOING TO DIE IN THE SAME SPOT AS THE PIRATE KING!!!
NOW WE WILL HOLD YOUR PUBLIC EXECUTION!!!

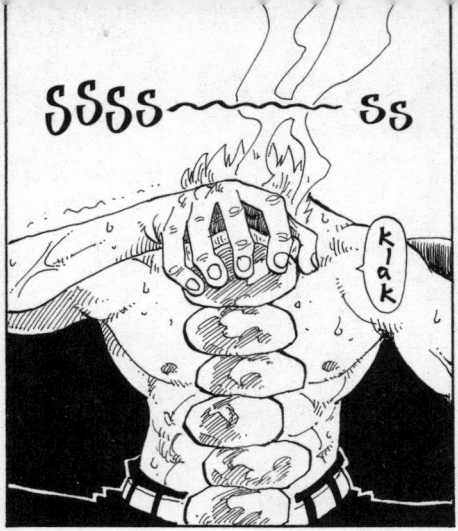
SSSS~~~~~~SS
klak

CAPTAIN SMOKER!! TERRIBLE NEWS!!!
MARINE

!
KLUNK
KRAK!!
WANTED
KLUNK KLUNK!!
PIRATES ARE CAUSING A DISTURBANCE AT THE EXECUTION SCAFFOLD!!!

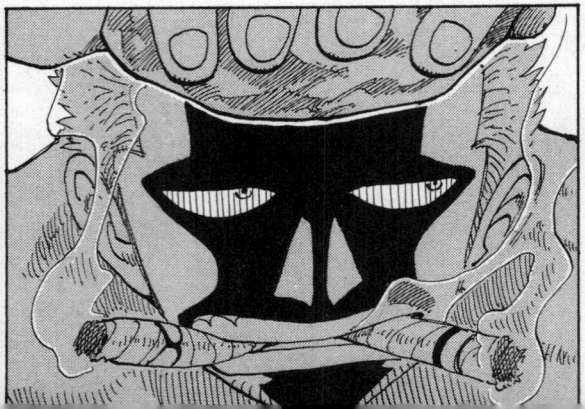

UH ...
THE PIRATES ARE-- !!

I SHOULDN'T RUSH IT...
...NOW SHOULD I?
-:CHOMP:-
NO GOOD. I'M TRYING TOO HARD.
WELL? WHAT HAPPENED?
YES, SIR...BEG PARDON, SIR.
KLAK!
OH YES, PIRATES ARE CAUSING A RUCKUS AT THE EXECUTION SCAFFOLD, EH?
UMM... WELL...
KLOMP KLOMP
KLOMP
HAVE THE REMAINING SOLDIERS TAKE UP POSITIONS WITHIN FIRING DISTANCE OF THE SQUARE.
HAVE SQUADRON TWO SURROUND THE AREA FROM THE ROAD TO THE SQUARE.
SEND SQUADRON ONE TO THE PORT.
Y-YES, SIR.
"WHITE CHASE" SMOKER
CAPTAIN, NAVY HEADQUARTERS

WH UMP!!
SPLAT!!
OH!

DON'T RUN OR YOU'LL DROP THEM.
WOW! THREE SCOOPS!!
TMP
TMP TMP
L AKA M

SHE'S JUST A LITTLE GIRL!!!

CAP-TAIN ...
PLEASE FOR-GIVE US!!
SHIUP
C-CAPTAIN SMOKER !!

M-MY...
...ICE CREAM ...

MY PANTS ATE UP ALL YOUR ICE CREAM.
NEXT TIME, TRY FIVE SCOOPS.
SORRY...
KLINK!

WHAP...
SHIVER!!
!!

MASTER CHIEF, HERE'S YOUR JACKET.
I'M SORRY!! I'LL GET READY RIGHT AWAY!
OH, THANK YOU, CHIEF.
TASHIGI!!! WHERE HAVE YOU BEEN!!?
CAPTAIN SMOKER, SORRY I'M LATE!!
OH...THANK YOU. I'M SO SORRY.
TMP TMP TMP TMP
LAKAM
YOU MEAN MORE SO THAN USUAL!!?
FOR-GIVE ME.
I'M A LITTLE OFF TODAY.
YES, SIR!
C'MON. THERE'S A DISTURBANCE AT THE SQUARE!!
MASTER CHIEF PETTY OFFICER TASHIGI
NAVY HEADQUARTERS

TMP TMP
...HAS THINNED OUT A LOT.
THE CROWD...
21

WHY DO I HAVE TO CARRY THE HEAVY END!?
YOU CAME ALONG AT JUST THE RIGHT TIME, USOPP.
BY THE WAY, I SAW A STRANGELY DRESSED MAN RIDING A LION EARLIER.

I'D BETTER RETURN TO THE SHIP RIGHT AWAY.
THE AIR PRESSURE HAS DROPPED DANGER-OUSLY LOW.

HUH?
BA-
AH.
DUMP
OH.
!!

ISN'T IT SUPPOSED TO BE RIGHT HERE?
HE SAID HE WANTED TO SEE THE EXECUTION SCAFFOLD.
SO? WHERE IS HE?

THERE ARE THREE WANTED INDIVIDUALS IN THE SQUARE.
A CIVILIAN'S BEING HELD HOSTAGE.
WHAT'S GOING ON HERE?
CAPTAIN!! MASTER CHIEF!!
THIRTY MILLION!! BEEN A WHILE SINCE WE HAD ONE LIKE THAT.
WE JUST GOT WORD A FEW DAYS AGO. HE HAS 30 MILLION BERRIES ON HIS HEAD.
LUFFY!? NEVER HEARD OF HIM.
!?
AND MONKEY D. LUFFY.
BUGGY THE CLOWN...
IRON MACE ALVIDA ...
DO
OH!!
... ABOUT TO BE KILLED !!
WELL...
...RIGHT NOW HE'S...
DARN! MY NOSE ITCHES.
DO OH!
LUFFY'S ON THE EXECUTION SCAFFOLD!!!?
WHAT !!?

7.

Luffy's Special Seat

- Captain's chair
- Luffy seems to like this chair. He's always sitting in it.

- He can't swim, so why would he sit in a spot like this? Who knows? But he seems happy, so what's wrong with that?

8.

Nami's Tangerine Grove

- When Nami left Coco Village, she took three of Belle-Mère's tangerine trees with her.
- Nami tends this little orchard.

- But Sanji's the one who protects the trees from tangerine snatchers (like Luffy).
- The tangerines are supposed to be very sweet.

Chapter 99: LUFFY DIED

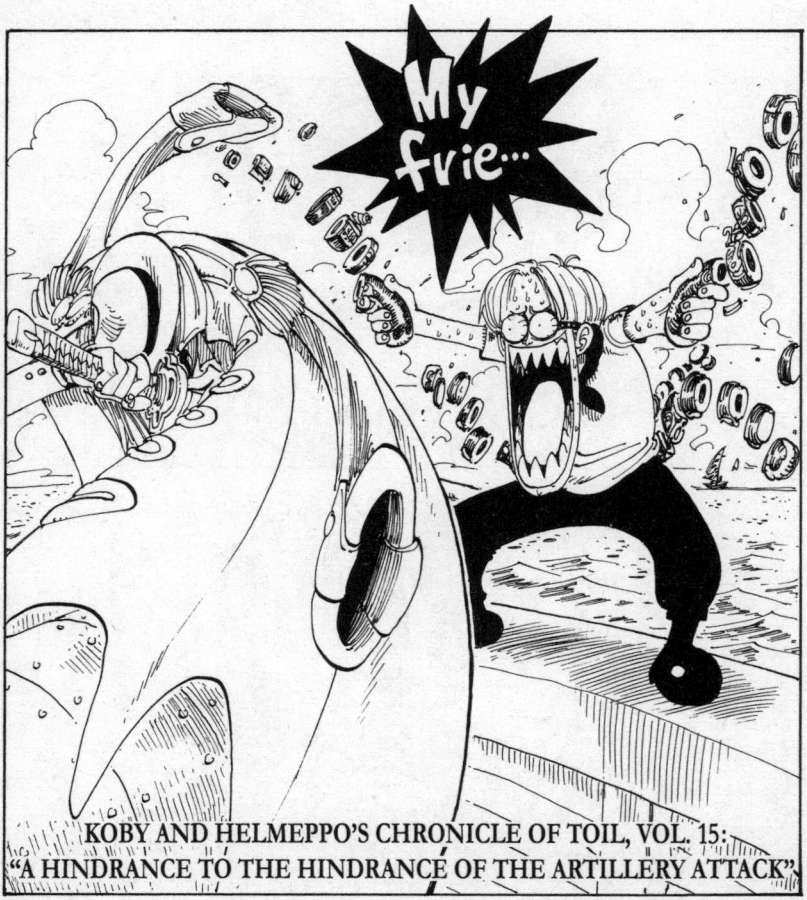

KOBY AND HELMEPPO'S CHRONICLE OF TOIL, VOL. 15:
"A HINDRANCE TO THE HINDRANCE OF THE ARTILLERY ATTACK"

WOOOO
...WERE EVENTS THAT TOOK PLACE IN THE DISTANT PAST.
LEGENDS THAT ENDURE IN THE FUTURE...
DOOM!!
FOR THAT, HE WILL BE EXECUTED IN GRAND STYLE!!!
THE CRIMINAL, M.D. LUFFY, IS GUILTY OF GETTING ON HIS HIGH HORSE AND UPSETTING ME!
BWAH HA HA HA HA HA HA
HOLD IT RIGHT THERE, YOU PIRATES!!!
HOORAY!!
SO CHEER IN GRAND STYLE!!!
BANG! BANGBANG!!!

YOU STOP JOKING AROUND!!!
HEY!! STOP JOKING AROUND !!!
THOOM!!
VEEN!!
YOU'RE THE ONE BEING EXECUTED !!!!
I'VE NEVER SEEN AN EXECUTION BEFORE.
THOOM!!
DOOM!!!
...THE GRAND-STYLE EXECU-TION!!!!
AND NOW, WE WILL COMMENCE WITH ...
NO-O-O !!!
BWAH
HA HA HA HA
BELL100

WE HAVE BIGGER FISH TO FRY RIGHT NOW.
WE COULD HELP HIM!! AFTER ALL, I DID KILL ONE OF THE BIG FISH OF THE FISH-MEN!!
WHAT GOOD CAN WE DO THERE!?
BIGGER FISH?
Big Fish

HEY, WHAT'S THE BIG RUSH!?
RRMMMBB..
WE SHOULD GO BACK TO THE SQUARE AND HELP LUFFY!

WHAT !!?
A STORM'S GOING TO HIT THIS ISLAND.

HEY!! WAIT UP!!!
OH! THIS REALLY IS IMPORTANT!!
THWUMP!!

IF THERE'S A COMMOTION IN THE SQUARE, THERE'LL BE SOLDIERS.
THIS IS THE CALM BEFORE THE STORM!!
AND I SAW DARK CLOUDS IN THE EASTERN SKY.
THE AIR PRESSURE AND TEMPERATURE HAVE BEEN STEADILY DROPPING.
...WHAT'LL WE DO IF WE TRY TO ESCAPE AND THE BOAT'S GONE!!?

CAPTAIN BUGGY HAS PROBABLY EXECUTED HIM IN GRAND STYLE BY NOW.
RARR!
Krsh Krsh
THIS IS THE RUBBER MAN'S SHIP.
IT'S BIGGER THAN BEFORE.
WHO'S THE ONE THAT RIDES THE RICHIE BIKE?
TELL ME, TELL ME WHO IT IS!!
IT'S ME. ♪
HEH HEH HEH...
HOWEVER, IF THE RUBBER MAN ESCAPES, WHICH IS IMPOSSIBLE...
SHIK...
BUT IF HE WERE TO ESCAPE SOMEHOW, IT'S OUR JOB TO...
...BURN HIS SHIP. ♪
RARR
RARR RARR...

A DISPUTE BETWEEN PIRATES, EH?
SHOULD WE ATTACK, SIR?
WHAT'S YOUR HURRY, FOOL?
BUT IF WE WAIT...

HAVE WE EVER ...
RRMMMBB...
...LET A PIRATE ESCAPE FROM OUR CITY?

N-NO, NEVER!!
THEN SHUT UP.
WE'LL LET THOSE PIRATES KILL EACH OTHER.
IT'LL MAKE OUR JOB EASY!!
NOW LISTEN, WHEN LUFFY'S HEAD ROLLS...
...SURROUND BUGGY, ALVIDA AND THE REST OF THEM.

IDIOT! AS IF I'D SPARE YOU!!!
PLEASE DON'T KILL ME!
I'M SORRY!
I'll never do it again.
WOOOO

SO MUCH FOR THE MAN I WAS GOING TO...
HMPH. THIS IS WHAT HAPPENS TO THOSE WHO DEFY US.

AW WELL, NEVER MIND THAT.
...
NO ONE WANTS TO HEAR IT.

YOU HAVE A BIG AUDIENCE.
ANY LAST WORDS?
...

THOOOM
I...
DOOO
...AM GOING TO BE KING OF THE PIRATES !!!!
!!!?
OOM

WHAT A DREAMER.
HERE, OF ALL PLACES?
POOF
THOOM
DID HE SAY "KING OF THE PIRATES" !!?
WHAT !!?
AAH
AAHEEK
EEEK
STOP THE EXECU-TION !!!!
!
WHAM
UGH!! U-UGH !!!
WHAM!!
IS THAT ALL YOU HAVE TO SAY, RUBBERHEAD!!?
BUT YOU'RE A SECOND TOO LATE!!
SO YOU'VE COME, ZOLO.
SANJI!!! ZOLO!!!
HELP!!!

IT'S RORONOA ZOLO!
WHAT'S GOING ON!?

...AND HIS PIRATES!!!
ZOLO'S WORKING WITH THAT MONKEY GUY...
WHAT!!?

ER... BUT...
THE BOUNTY HUNTER? WHAT GREAT TIMING!!

RORONOA ZOLO!? HERE!?

IT'S THAT GUY!!!
!!!

GOT IT!!
TEAR DOWN THE SCAFFOLD!!
EEEK
AAAH
AAAH

WE'LL WIPE THEM OUT, LADY ALVIDA!!!
GET 'EM, MEN !!!
YARR!!
SHEEN...
THWAK THWAK THWAK
OOF!
UGH!
OUTTA MY WAY !!!
HA HA HA HA HA HA HA HA
YOUR CAPTAIN IS DEAD!!!
...
BWAH HA HA HA HA!! YOU CAN SEE THE WHOLE THING FROM OVER THERE !!!

THWAK THWAK!!!
FIGHT!!!
DARN YOU!!!
UGH!
GAH!!!
IF I CAN JUST KICK DOWN THE PLATFORM!!!
...!!!
RR
BB
WHAM WHAM WHAM WHAM!!!
IF I CAN JUST CHOP DOWN THE PLATFORM!!!
NAMI!!
USOPP!!
HURRY!!
IT'S HEAVY!!
SANJI!!
ZOLO!!
AAH
AAH
YES, SIR!!
PREPARE FOR BATTLE.
WHUP

I'M A GONER.
SORRY.
RRMMBB...
HEE !!
!!!
DON'T TALK CRAZY!!!
NO!
KRAK
KRAK!!!
HE LAUGHED.

KRAK KRAK!!!
DOOM!!!

KRAK
!!!?
PLIP
PLIP
PLIP
PLUP
PLUP
PLUP
SSSS
KSHHHH...!!
KRASH!!

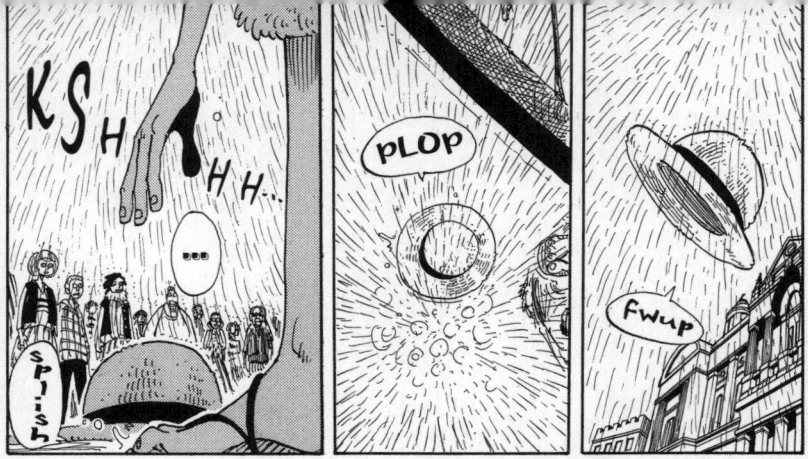
KSHHH...
...
SPLISH
PLOP
FWUP

LUCKY ME.
SPLOP
HA HA HA HA! I'M ALIVE.

KSHHHHH...!

DON'T TALK NONSENSE. LET'S GET OUTTA HERE.
WE'RE NOT IN THE CLEAR YET.
KLANK
THANK GOOD-NESS.
DO YOU BELIEVE IN A HIGHER POWER?
RAAAH
RUN FOR IT !!!
HEY, WHICH WAY!?
HERE THEY COME !!
SURROUND THE SQUARE AND CAPTURE THE PIRATES!!
DOOM!!
HE SAW HIS DEATH, ACCEPTED IT AND LAUGHED!!
IN THAT MOMENT HE ACCEPTED HIS FATE.
THAT'S NOT IT!!!
WHY DID HE LAUGH? DID HE KNOW HE'D BE RESCUED?

WELL, THAT MONKEY LAUGHED!!!
...EVERY MAN TREMBLES IN FEAR, HOWEVER TOUGH HE IS.
LAUGH!? WHEN FACED WITH CERTAIN DEATH...
SOLDIER, DID YOU EVER SEE A PIRATE LAUGH RIGHT BEFORE HIS EXECUTION?
CAPTAIN!! THE PIRATE ROUND-UP IS...
YACK
YACK

TWENTY-TWO YEARS AGO, ANOTHER MAN LAUGHED ON THAT VERY SPOT.
HE WAS GOLD ROGER, KING OF THE PIRATES!!!

WOOOOOO

THEY WENT BACK TO THE BASE FOR MORE.
THE SUDDEN DOWNPOUR WET THEIR GUNPOWDER.
WAIT, NO...
MARINE
THEN THE PORT IS UNPROTECTED!!!
HE WENT WEST.
WHICH WAY DID HE GO?
RAAAAAAAAH
THE FIRST SQUADRON SHOULD BE THERE.
IT'S AS THOUGH SOME KIND OF FORCE IS WILLING THIS MAN'S SURVIVAL !!!
CLENCH
IS THIS JUST A COINCIDENCE ...!!?
WOOO
THE WIND IS BLOWING TOWARD THE WEST. THEY'LL HAVE A TAILWIND.
I WILL NOT LET HIM LEAVE THIS ISLAND !!!
I, "WHITE CHASE" SMOKER, STAKE MY REPUTATION AS CAPTAIN OF THIS BATTALION.
TO BE CONTINUED IN ONE PIECE, VOL. 12!

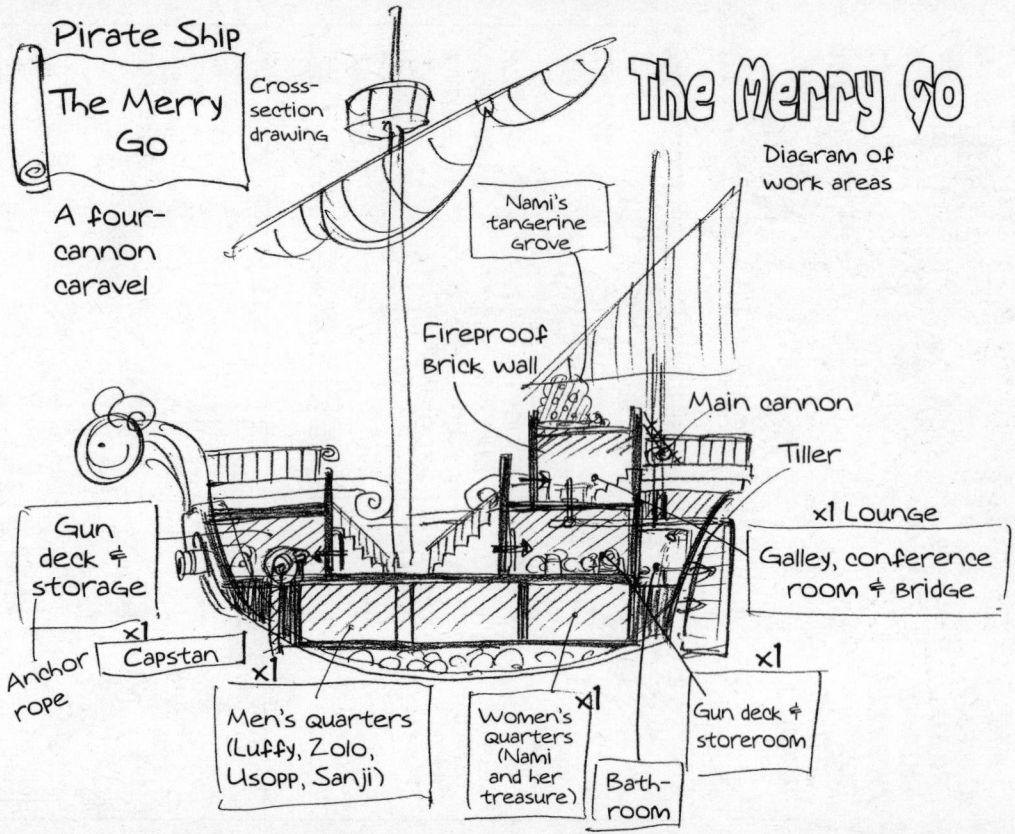
Pirate Ship
The Merry Go
Cross-section drawing
The Merry Go
Diagram of work areas
A four-cannon caravel
Nami's tangerine grove
Fireproof brick wall
Main cannon
Tiller
x1 Lounge
Galley, conference room & bridge
Gun deck & storage
x1
Capstan
Anchor rope
x1
Men's quarters (Luffy, Zolo, Usopp, Sanji)
Women's quarters (Nami and her treasure)
x1
Bath-room
x1
Gun deck & storeroom

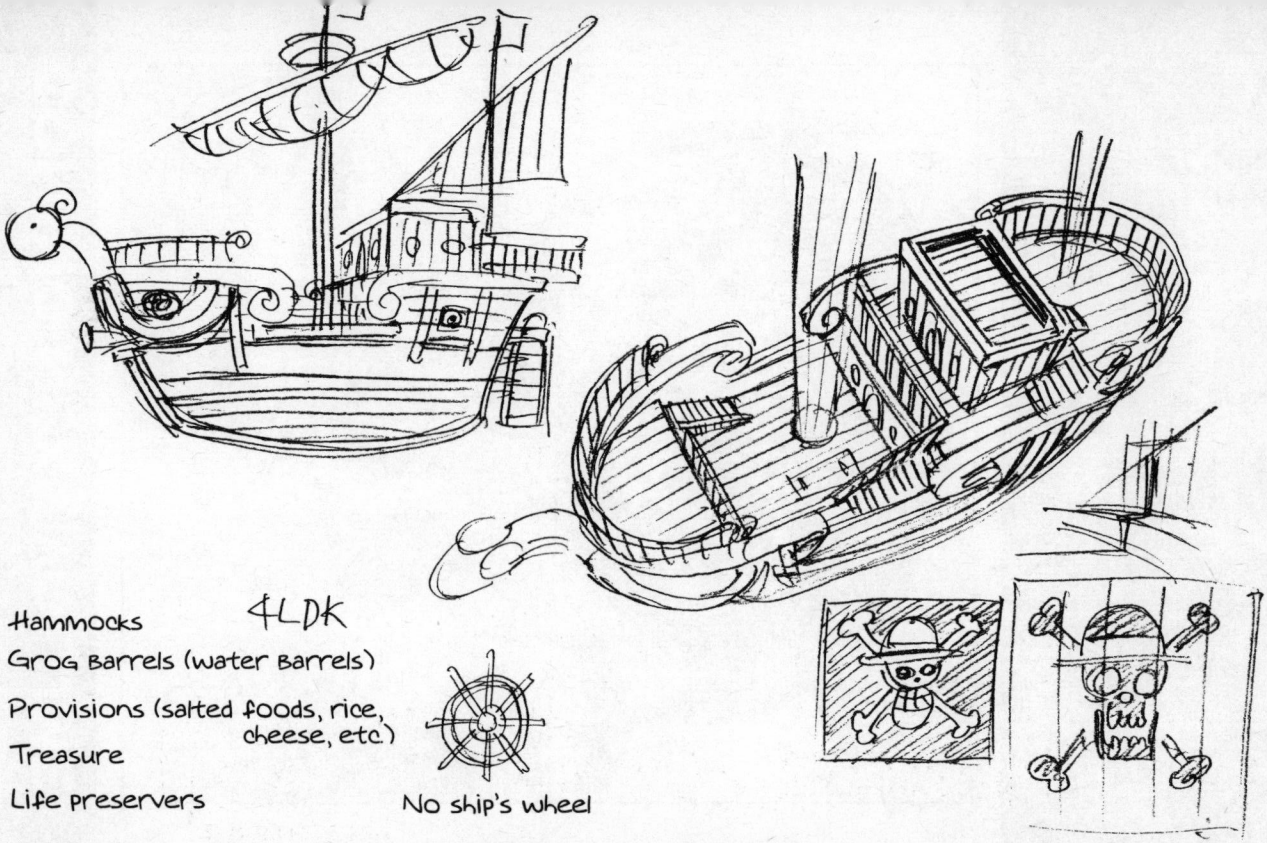
Hammocks
4LDK
Grog Barrels (water Barrels)
Provisions (salted foods, rice, cheese, etc.)
Treasure
Life preservers
No ship's wheel

COMING NEXT VOLUME:

Luffy and his crew are bound for the Grand Line at last, with both newfound enemies and old ones in hot pursuit. Braving a terrible storm, the Straw Hat Pirates make their way toward what they believe is the entrance to the famed sea. But Nami's map is pointing straight up the side of a mountain!

ON SALE NOW!

WHEN NIGHT FALLS, THE YOKAI KING WILL RISE.

NURA: RISE OF THE YOKAI CLAN

BY HIROSHI SHIIBASHI

YOU'VE SEEN THE ANIME NOW READ THE MANGA

ISBN-13: 978-1-4215-3891-4
US $9.99 CAN $12.99

Watch the Anime @ VIZAnime.com

SHONEN JUMP MANGA
www.shonenjump.viz.com

Pre-Order now at store.viz.com
Also available at your local bookstore or comic store

NURARIHYON NO MAGO © 2008 by Hiroshi Shiibashi/SHUEISHA Inc.

RATED T FOR TEEN ratings.viz.com

viz media
www.viz.com
VIZ ANIME

PHONE IN AND THEN...

...FIGHT TO GET OUT!

From the pages of *SHONEN JUMP* Magazine!

PSYREN

Story and Art by Toshiaki Iwashiro

Ageha Yoshina just got transported to a warped alternate dimension where you've got to fight your way back to our world— or die trying.

ISBN-13: 978-1-4215-3676-7

$9.99 US | $12.99 CAN

SHONEN JUMP MANGA

www.shonenjump.com

On sale now at www.viz.com

Also available at your local bookstore or comic store.

PSYREN © 2007 by Toshiaki Iwashiro/SHUEISHA Inc.

RATED T FOR TEEN ratings.viz.com

viz media

www.viz.com

BAKUMAN。

STORY BY TSUGUMI OHBA
ART BY TAKESHI OBATA

From the creators of *Death Note*

The mystery behind manga making REVEALED!

Average student Moritaka Mashiro enjoys drawing for fun. When his classmate and aspiring writer Akito Takagi discovers his talent, he begs to team up. But what exactly does it take to make it in the manga-publishing world?

Bakuman。, Vol. 1
ISBN: 978-1-4215-3513-5
$9.99 US / $12.99 CAN *

Manga on sale at store.viz.com
Also available at your local bookstore or comic store

www.shonenjump.com

BAKUMAN。 © 2008 by Tsugumi Ohba, Takeshi Obata/SHUEISHA Inc.
* Prices subject to change

www.viz.com

VIZMANGA

Read manga anytime, anywhere!

From our newest hit series to the classics you know and love, the best manga in the world is now available digitally. Buy a volume* of digital manga for your:

- iOS device (**iPad®, iPhone®, iPod® touch**) through the **VIZ Manga app**
- Android-powered device (**phone or tablet**) with a browser by visiting VIZManga.com
- **Mac or PC computer** by visiting VIZManga.com

VIZ Digital has loads to offer:

- 500+ ready-to-read volumes
- New volumes each week
- FREE previews
- Access on multiple devices! Create a log-in through the app so you buy a book once, and read it on your device of choice!*

To learn more, visit www.viz.com/apps

*** Some series may not be available for multiple devices. Check the app on your device to find out what's available.**

DEATH NOTE © 2003 by Tsugumi Ohba, Takeshi Obata/SHUEISHA Inc.
NURARIHYON NO MAGO © 2008 by Hiroshi Shiibashi/SHUEISHA Inc.
ONE PIECE © 1997 by Eiichiro Oda/SHUEISHA Inc.

viz.com/apps

DISCOVER ANIME

IN A WHOLE NEW WAY!

www.neonalley.com

What it is...

- Streaming anime delivered 24/7 straight to your TV via your connected video game console
- All English dubbed content
- Anime, martial arts movies, and more

Go to **neonalley.com** for news, updates and to see if Neon Alley is available in your area.

NEON ALLEY is a trademark or service mark of VIZ Media, LLC

You're Reading in the Wrong Direction!!

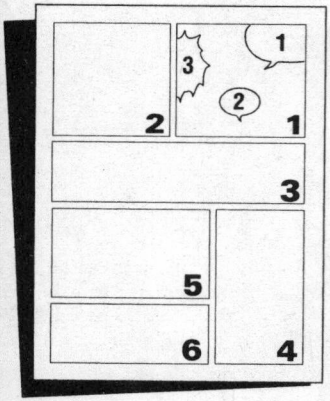

Whoops! Guess what? You're starting at the wrong end of the comic!

...It's true! In keeping with the original Japanese format, **One Piece** is meant to be read from right to left, starting in the upper-right corner.

Unlike English, which is read from left to right, Japanese is read from right to left, meaning that action, sound effects and word-balloon order are completely reversed... something which can make readers unfamiliar with Japanese feel pretty backwards themselves. For this reason, manga or Japanese comics published in the U.S. in English have sometimes been published "flopped"—that is, printed in exact reverse order, as though seen from the other side of a mirror.

By flopping pages, U.S. publishers can avoid confusing readers, but the compromise is not without its downside. For one thing, a character in a flopped manga series who once wore in the original Japanese version a T-shirt emblazoned with "M A Y" (as in "the merry month of") now wears one which reads "Y A M"! Additionally, many manga creators in Japan are themselves unhappy with the process, as some feel the mirror-imaging of their art skews their original intentions.

We are proud to bring you Eiichiro Oda's **One Piece** in the original unflopped format. For now, though, turn to the other side of the book and let the journey begin...!

—Editor